Tab 1

CrewAI Simplified

The Beginner's Path to Building Multi-Agent AI Systems

Henry Finley

Copyright © 2024 by Henry Finley

All rights reserved.

No part of this publication may be reproduced, distributed, or transmitted in any form or by any means, including photocopying, recording, or other electronic or mechanical methods, without the prior written permission of the publisher, except in the case of brief quotations embodied in critical reviews and certain other non commercial uses permitted by copyright law.

Table of contents

Preface — 6
Part I — 7
Understanding CrewAI and Collaborative AI Basics — 7
Chapter 1: Introduction to CrewAI — 8
   1.1 What is CrewAI? — 8
   1.2 The Rise of Collaborative AI Systems — 9
   1.3 Why CrewAI Matters in Today's AI Landscape — 10
   1.4 Overview of CrewAI Use Cases — 12
Chapter 2: The Foundations of Collaborative AI — 14
   2.1 What is Collaborative AI? — 14
   2.2 Differences Between Traditional AI and Collaborative AI — 15
   2.3 Key Components of a Collaborative AI System — 17
   2.4 Benefits and Challenges of Collaborative AI — 18
Chapter 3 Key Concepts in CrewAI — 20
   3.1 Roles within CrewAI Systems — 20
   3.2 Communication and Coordination in CrewAI — 21
   3.3 Task Assignment and Load Balancing — 25
   3.4 Ethical and Security Considerations in Collaboration — 30
Part II — 32
Setting Up CrewAI Systems — 32
Chapter 4 Getting Started with CrewAI Tools — 33
   4.1 Overview of Popular CrewAI Tools and Platforms — 33
   4.2 Installation and Setup Guides — 35
   4.3 Choosing the Right Tools for Your Needs — 37
   4.4 Basic Setup for a Collaborative AI Project — 39
Chapter 5 Building Your First CrewAI Workflow — 42
   5.1 Defining Goals and Requirements — 42
   5.2 Creating a Simple Task Flow — 44
   5.3 Integrating Multiple AI Agents for a Common Task — 46
   5.4 Hands-On Example: A Basic CrewAI Project — 53
Chapter 6 Configuring Communication and Task

Coordination   **58**
    6.1 How AI Agents Communicate and Collaborate   58
    6.2 Setting Up Messaging Protocols   59
    6.3 Task Distribution Strategies   62
    6.4 Examples of Communication Models in Action   64

Chapter 7 Data Sharing and Processing in CrewAI   **67**
    7.1 Understanding Data Flow and Sharing   67
    7.2 Data Integration and Compatibility Issues   68
    7.3 Best Practices for Secure Data Handling   70
    7.4 Examples of Data Sharing Mechanisms   72

Part III   **75**
Core Techniques for Collaborative AI   **75**

Chapter 8: Agent Role Specialization   **76**
    8.1 What is Role Specialization in CrewAI?   76
    8.2 Setting Up Specialized Agents for Different Tasks   77
    8.3 Balancing Flexibility and Specialization   79
    8.4 Real-World Examples of Role Specialization   80

Chapter 9 Workflow Management in CrewAI Systems   **82**
    9.1 Principles of Effective Workflow Management   82
    9.2 Monitoring Task Progress and Agent Performance   83
    9.3 Dynamic Adjustment of Workflows   87
    9.4 Tools for Tracking and Optimization   88

Chapter 10 Conflict Resolution in Collaborative AI   **91**
    10.1 Identifying Potential Conflicts Between Agents   91
    10.2 Techniques for Resolving Agent Disputes   92
    10.3 Managing Overlapping Tasks and Priorities   94
    10.4 Case Study: Conflict Resolution in Practice   96

Chapter 11 Training and Improving AI Agents   **98**
    11.1 Reinforcement Learning Techniques for Agent Training   98
    11.2 Transfer Learning and Fine-Tuning Pre-trained Models   100
    11.3 Continuous Learning and Adaptation in Dynamic Environments   104

Part IV   **107**
Practical Applications of CrewAI   **107**

Chapter 12 CrewAI in Business and Industry — 108
- 12.1 How CrewAI is Transforming Different Sectors — 108
- 12.2 Applications in Ecommerce, Customer Support, and Operations — 109
- 12.3 Case Studies of Successful CrewAI Implementations — 111

Chapter 13 Advanced Use Cases in Research and Development — 113
- 13.1 Using CrewAI for Scientific Research and Data Analysis — 113
- 13.2 Collaborative AI for Innovation and Prototyping — 114
- 13.3 Real-World Examples from Leading Research Labs — 116

Chapter 14 Developing Custom CrewAI Solutions — 118
- 14.1 When to Build Custom Solutions vs. Using Out-of-the-Box Tools — 118
- 14.2 Introduction to Customizing Agents for Specific Tasks — 119
- 14.3 Integrating CrewAI with Other Business Systems — 121
- 14.4 Example of a Customized CrewAI Solution — 122

Part V — 125
Best Practices and Future Directions — 125

Chapter 15 Best Practices for CrewAI Success — 126
- 15.1 Tips for Effective Collaboration and Efficiency — 126
- 15.2 Managing Resource Use and Cost Efficiency — 127
- 15.3 Improving Agent Communication and Coordination — 129
- 15.4 Security and Privacy Best Practices — 131

Chapter 16 Ethical and Social Considerations — 133
- 16.1 Addressing Bias and Fairness in CrewAI Systems — 133
- 16.2 Privacy and Data Protection in Collaborative AI — 134
- 16.3 Ensuring Transparency and Accountability — 136
- 16.4 Ethical Case Studies and Best Practices — 137

Chapter 17 Monitoring and Debugging CrewAI Systems — 140
- 17.1 Identifying and Troubleshooting Common Issues — 140
- 17.2 Monitoring Agent Performance and System Health — 142
- 17.3 Debugging Techniques for Collaborative AI Systems — 143

Chapter 18 Human-AI Collaboration — 146
- 18.1 Designing Effective Human-AI Interfaces — 146

 18.2 Enhancing Human-AI Teamwork   149
 18.3 Leveraging Human Expertise to Improve AI Performance 151
Chapter 19: The Future of Collaborative AI and CrewAI 153
 19.1 Trends in AI Collaboration and Future Applications   153
 19.2 Innovations and Emerging Technologies in CrewAI   155
 19.3 How to Stay Updated on Advances in Collaborative AI   156
 19.4 Final Thoughts on CrewAI for Beginners   158
Appendix   **160**
 A.1 Glossary of Key Terms   160
 A.2 Additional Resources and Recommended Reading   161
 A.3 Index   163
Conclusion   **165**

Preface

Imagine a world where AI agents, working together seamlessly, can solve complex problems, from accelerating medical research to optimizing global supply chains. This is the world of CrewAI.

Why should you care about CrewAI?

- **Revolutionizing Industries:** CrewAI is reshaping industries like healthcare, finance, and manufacturing, driving innovation and efficiency.
- **Solving Global Challenges:** From climate change to poverty, CrewAI can help us address some of the world's most pressing issues.
- **Personalizing Experiences:** CrewAI can tailor experiences to individual needs, from personalized recommendations to customized learning.

This book is your guide to the exciting world of CrewAI.

We'll explore the fundamental concepts, practical techniques, and real-world applications of CrewAI. You'll learn how to:

- Design and develop collaborative AI systems
- Train and optimize AI agents
- Manage complex workflows and resolve conflicts
- Ensure ethical and responsible AI development

Whether you're a seasoned AI practitioner or a curious beginner, this book will provide you with the knowledge and tools you need to succeed.

Let's embark on this journey together and shape the future of AI.

Part I
Understanding CrewAI and Collaborative AI Basics

Chapter 1: Introduction to CrewAI

1.1 What is CrewAI?

CrewAI is a groundbreaking concept in the realm of artificial intelligence that empowers multiple AI agents to collaborate and work together towards a common goal. It's like a team of AI experts, each with their own unique skills, coming together to solve complex problems.

Imagine a scenario: A self-driving car. It's not just one AI model making all the decisions. Instead, it's a team of AI agents: one focusing on traffic prediction, another on pedestrian detection, and yet another on obstacle avoidance. They work in harmony, sharing information and making joint decisions to ensure a safe and efficient journey.

This is the essence of CrewAI. It's about creating intelligent systems that can:

- **Collaborate effectively:** AI agents can communicate and coordinate their actions.
- **Share knowledge and resources:** Information can be exchanged and pooled to enhance decision-making.
- **Adapt to changing circumstances:** The system can dynamically adjust to new situations and challenges.
- **Learn and improve over time:** AI agents can learn from their experiences and become more intelligent.

Key Benefits of CrewAI:

- **Enhanced problem-solving:** By combining the strengths of multiple AI agents, CrewAI can tackle more complex problems.
- **Increased efficiency:** Collaborative AI can optimize resource utilization and reduce processing time.
- **Improved decision-making:** By sharing information and perspectives, AI agents can make more informed decisions.

- **Greater robustness:** A diverse team of AI agents can increase the system's resilience to failures and errors.

In the following chapters, we'll delve deeper into the technical aspects of CrewAI, explore real-world applications, and discuss the ethical implications of this powerful technology.

1.2 The Rise of Collaborative AI Systems

The concept of artificial intelligence has been rapidly evolving, and we're witnessing a shift from individual AI agents to collaborative AI systems. This trend is driven by several factors:

1. The Limits of Individual AI Agents:

- **Complexity of Real-World Problems:** Many real-world problems are multifaceted and require a nuanced approach. A single AI agent may struggle to handle the complexity and uncertainty inherent in such scenarios.
- **Data Scarcity and Bias:** AI models often rely on large amounts of data to learn effectively. However, data scarcity and bias can limit the performance of individual AI agents.

2. The Power of Collaboration:

- **Shared Knowledge and Expertise:** By collaborating, AI agents can pool their knowledge and expertise, leading to more accurate and informed decisions.
- **Distributed Problem-Solving:** Collaborative AI systems can break down complex problems into smaller, more manageable subproblems, which can be solved by specialized AI agents.
- **Enhanced Adaptability:** Collaborative AI systems can adapt to changing environments and unexpected challenges more effectively than individual AI agents.

3. Technological Advancements:

- **Improved Communication Protocols:** Advances in communication protocols enable AI agents to exchange information and coordinate their actions seamlessly.

- **Powerful Hardware:** The increasing availability of powerful hardware, such as GPUs and TPUs, allows for the development of more complex and sophisticated AI systems.
- **Advanced Algorithms:** The development of advanced algorithms, such as reinforcement learning and multi-agent systems, has facilitated the creation of intelligent, collaborative AI agents.

As we move forward, we can expect to see even more sophisticated collaborative AI systems that can revolutionize various industries, from healthcare to finance and beyond. By understanding the underlying principles and benefits of collaborative AI, we can harness its potential to create a better future.

1.3 Why CrewAI Matters in Today's AI Landscape

CrewAI is emerging as a critical paradigm shift in the field of artificial intelligence. It offers a promising approach to tackling complex problems that traditional AI methods may struggle with. Here's why CrewAI matters in today's AI landscape:

1. Real-World Complexity:

- **Multifaceted Problems:** Many real-world problems, such as climate change, healthcare, and urban planning, involve multiple interconnected factors. A single AI agent may not be sufficient to address the complexity and scale of these challenges.
- **Dynamic Environments:** Real-world environments are constantly changing, and AI systems must be able to adapt quickly to new situations. Collaborative AI systems can respond more effectively to these dynamic conditions.

2. Enhanced Performance and Efficiency:

- **Synergistic Collaboration:** By working together, AI agents can leverage their collective intelligence to achieve better results than they could individually.

- **Efficient Resource Utilization:** Collaborative AI systems can optimize resource allocation and reduce computational costs.
- **Improved Decision-Making:** By sharing information and perspectives, AI agents can make more informed decisions, leading to better outcomes.

3. **Ethical Considerations and Bias Mitigation:**

- **Diverse Perspectives:** A diverse team of AI agents can help mitigate bias and ensure fairness in decision-making.
- **Ethical Guidelines:** Collaborative AI systems can be designed to adhere to ethical principles and avoid unintended consequences.

4. **Future Innovations:**

- **Human-AI Collaboration:** CrewAI can facilitate seamless collaboration between humans and AI, leading to innovative solutions.
- **Autonomous Systems:** Collaborative AI systems can power autonomous systems, such as self-driving cars and drones.
- **AI-Powered Creativity:** AI agents can work together to generate creative ideas and content.

CrewAI represents a significant advancement in the field of AI. By understanding its principles and applications, we can unlock its potential to address some of the most pressing challenges facing humanity.

1.4 Overview of CrewAI Use Cases

CrewAI has the potential to revolutionize numerous industries. Here are some of the most promising use cases:

Healthcare

- **Medical Diagnosis:** Multiple AI agents can analyze medical images, patient records, and genetic data to identify diseases more accurately and efficiently.

- **Drug Discovery:** AI agents can collaborate to accelerate drug discovery processes by simulating molecular interactions and predicting drug efficacy.
- **Personalized Treatment Plans:** AI agents can analyze patient data to develop personalized treatment plans tailored to individual needs.

Finance

- **Fraud Detection:** AI agents can work together to identify fraudulent transactions by analyzing various data sources, such as transaction history, IP addresses, and user behavior.
- **Algorithmic Trading:** AI agents can collaborate to make complex trading decisions in real-time, optimizing investment portfolios.
- **Risk Assessment:** AI agents can assess financial risks by analyzing market trends, economic indicators, and company performance data.

Autonomous Systems

- **Self-Driving Cars:** Multiple AI agents can collaborate to handle various aspects of autonomous driving, such as perception, planning, and control.
- **Drones:** AI agents can work together to perform tasks such as delivery, surveillance, and search and rescue.
- **Robotics:** AI agents can collaborate to perform complex tasks in manufacturing, logistics, and healthcare.

Climate Science

- **Climate Modeling:** AI agents can analyze vast amounts of climate data to improve climate models and predict future climate trends.
- **Natural Disaster Prediction:** AI agents can identify patterns in data to predict natural disasters, such as hurricanes, earthquakes, and wildfires.

- **Sustainable Energy:** AI agents can optimize energy consumption and production by analyzing energy usage patterns and predicting future demand.

These are just a few examples of the many potential applications of CrewAI. As the technology continues to advance, we can expect to see even more innovative and impactful use cases emerge.

Chapter 2: The Foundations of Collaborative AI

2.1 What is Collaborative AI?

Collaborative AI is a paradigm shift in artificial intelligence where multiple AI agents work together to solve complex problems. Unlike traditional AI, which often relies on single, isolated agents, collaborative AI fosters cooperation and information sharing among multiple agents. This approach enables AI systems to tackle more challenging tasks, make more informed decisions, and adapt to changing environments.

Key Characteristics of Collaborative AI:

- **Multiple Agents:** Collaborative AI systems involve multiple AI agents, each with its own capabilities and responsibilities.
- **Communication and Coordination:** Agents must be able to communicate and coordinate their actions to achieve a common goal.
- **Shared Knowledge and Resources:** Agents can share information, data, and resources to improve their performance.
- **Emergent Behavior:** Sometimes, collaborative AI systems can exhibit emergent behavior, where the collective intelligence of the agents surpasses the sum of their individual capabilities.

The Power of Collaboration:

By working together, AI agents can:

- **Handle Complex Problems:** Collaborative AI systems can tackle complex problems that are beyond the scope of individual agents.
- **Improve Decision-Making:** By sharing information and perspectives, agents can make more informed and accurate decisions.

- **Enhance Adaptability:** Collaborative AI systems can adapt to changing environments and unexpected challenges more effectively.
- **Increase Efficiency:** By distributing tasks and sharing resources, collaborative AI systems can improve efficiency and reduce costs.

In the following sections, we will delve deeper into the key components of collaborative AI systems, the benefits they offer, and the challenges they present.

2.2 Differences Between Traditional AI and Collaborative AI

While traditional AI and collaborative AI share the goal of creating intelligent systems, they differ significantly in their approach and capabilities.

Traditional AI

- **Single Agent:** Relies on a single AI agent to perform tasks independently.
- **Limited Problem-Solving:** Often struggles with complex, real-world problems that require multiple perspectives and skills.
- **Static Environment:** Assumes a relatively static environment and may not adapt well to changes.
- **Limited Learning:** Primarily learns from historical data and may not be able to learn from new experiences in real-time.

Collaborative AI

- **Multiple Agents:** Involves multiple AI agents working together to solve problems.
- **Enhanced Problem-Solving:** Can handle complex problems by leveraging the combined intelligence of multiple agents.
- **Dynamic Adaptation:** Can adapt to changing environments and unexpected challenges.

- **Continuous Learning:** Agents can learn from each other and from new experiences, leading to improved performance over time.

Key Differences Summarized:

Feature	Traditional AI	Collaborative AI
Number of Agents	Single	Multiple
Problem-Solving Capability	Limited	Enhanced
Adaptability	Limited	High
Learning Ability	Limited	Continuous

By understanding the differences between traditional AI and collaborative AI, we can appreciate the potential of collaborative AI to revolutionize various industries and address complex challenges.

2.3 Key Components of a Collaborative AI System

A collaborative AI system typically consists of several key components:

1. AI Agents

- **Individual Agents:** These are the basic units of a collaborative AI system. Each agent has its own intelligence

and capabilities, such as perception, decision-making, and action-taking.
- **Specialized Agents:** Different agents can be specialized in specific tasks, such as data analysis, natural language processing, or image recognition.

2. Communication and Coordination

- **Communication Protocols:** Agents must be able to communicate with each other effectively. This involves using appropriate communication protocols and data formats.
- **Coordination Mechanisms:** Agents need mechanisms to coordinate their actions and avoid conflicts. This can be achieved through centralized control, decentralized coordination, or a combination of both.

3. Knowledge Sharing and Learning

- **Knowledge Base:** A shared knowledge base allows agents to access and share information.
- **Learning Mechanisms:** Agents can learn from each other and from their own experiences to improve their performance.

4. Task Allocation and Planning

- **Task Allocation:** Agents must be able to assign tasks to each other based on their capabilities and workload.
- **Planning:** Agents need to plan their actions and coordinate with other agents to achieve a common goal.

5. Conflict Resolution

- **Conflict Detection:** Agents must be able to detect potential conflicts in their plans and actions.
- **Conflict Resolution Strategies:** Agents need strategies to resolve conflicts, such as negotiation, arbitration, or compromise.

By understanding these key components, we can design and implement effective collaborative AI systems that can address complex challenges and achieve significant results.

2.4 Benefits and Challenges of Collaborative AI

Collaborative AI offers numerous benefits, but it also comes with certain challenges.

Benefits of Collaborative AI

- **Enhanced Problem-Solving:** By combining the strengths of multiple AI agents, collaborative AI can tackle complex problems that are beyond the capabilities of individual agents.
- **Improved Decision-Making:** Collaborative AI systems can make more informed decisions by sharing information and perspectives.
- **Increased Efficiency:** By distributing tasks and sharing resources, collaborative AI can improve efficiency and reduce costs.
- **Greater Adaptability:** Collaborative AI systems can adapt to changing environments and unexpected challenges more effectively.
- **Increased Creativity:** By working together, AI agents can generate new ideas and solutions.

Challenges of Collaborative AI

- **Complexity:** Designing and implementing collaborative AI systems can be complex, requiring careful consideration of factors such as communication, coordination, and conflict resolution.
- **Scalability:** As the number of agents increases, the complexity of managing and coordinating the system also increases.
- **Ethical Considerations:** Collaborative AI systems raise ethical concerns, such as privacy, security, and accountability.

- **Technical Challenges:** Challenges such as network latency, data privacy, and security can hinder the effective implementation of collaborative AI systems.

By understanding both the benefits and challenges of collaborative AI, we can develop effective strategies to maximize its potential while mitigating its risks.

Chapter 3 Key Concepts in CrewAI

3.1 Roles within CrewAI Systems

A CrewAI system typically involves three key roles: agents, controllers, and users.

1. Agents

- **Definition:** AI agents are the individual units within a CrewAI system. They are responsible for performing specific tasks and making decisions.
- **Types:**
    - **Specialized Agents:** These agents are designed to perform specific tasks, such as data analysis, natural language processing, or image recognition.
    - **General-Purpose Agents:** These agents are more versatile and can perform a wider range of tasks.
- **Responsibilities:**
    - **Task Execution:** Agents carry out assigned tasks.
    - **Communication:** Agents communicate with other agents and with the controller.
    - **Learning and Adaptation:** Agents can learn from their experiences and adapt to changing conditions.

2. Controllers

- **Definition:** Controllers oversee the overall operation of the CrewAI system.
- **Responsibilities:**
    - **Task Allocation:** Controllers assign tasks to agents based on their capabilities and workload.
    - **Monitoring and Control:** Controllers monitor the performance of agents and intervene if necessary.
    - **Conflict Resolution:** Controllers resolve conflicts between agents.

- **Learning and Adaptation:** Controllers can learn from the system's performance and adapt the system's behavior.

3. Users

- **Definition:** Users interact with the CrewAI system to provide input, receive output, and monitor the system's performance.
- **Responsibilities:**
    - **Task Definition:** Users define the goals and objectives of the CrewAI system.
    - **Data Input:** Users provide the necessary data for the agents to process.
    - **Output Interpretation:** Users interpret the output generated by the agents.
    - **System Monitoring:** Users monitor the system's performance and make adjustments as needed.

By understanding the roles of agents, controllers, and users, we can design and implement effective CrewAI systems that can address complex challenges.

3.2 Communication and Coordination in CrewAI

Effective communication and coordination are essential for the success of any collaborative AI system. In CrewAI, agents must be able to exchange information, share knowledge, and coordinate their actions to achieve a common goal.

Communication Protocols

- **Point-to-Point Communication:** Agents can communicate directly with each other. This is useful for simple tasks and for sharing information between specific agents.
- **Broadcast Communication:** Agents can broadcast messages to all other agents. This is useful for sharing global information or alerting other agents to potential threats.

- **Shared Memory:** Agents can access and modify a shared memory space. This is useful for sharing data and coordinating actions.

Coordination Mechanisms

- **Centralized Control:** A central controller coordinates the activities of all agents. This approach can be effective for simple systems, but it can become a bottleneck as the system grows in complexity.
- **Decentralized Control:** Agents coordinate their actions without a central controller. This approach is more scalable and resilient to failures, but it can be more challenging to implement.
- **Hybrid Approach:** A combination of centralized and decentralized control can be used to balance the benefits of both approaches.

Understanding the Concepts

- **Communication:** The process of exchanging information between agents.
- **Coordination:** The process of organizing and synchronizing the actions of multiple agents.

Real-World Analogy: A Soccer Team

A soccer team is a great example of a collaborative system. Players (agents) communicate through signals, gestures, and verbal cues to coordinate their movements and strategies. A successful team relies on effective communication and coordination to achieve their goal of scoring goals.

Step-by-Step Example: Centralized Communication and Coordination

Scenario: A fleet of drones delivering packages.

1. **Central Control:** A central control system oversees the entire operation.

2. **Task Assignment:** The central control system assigns delivery tasks to individual drones based on their location, battery level, and payload capacity.
3. **Communication:** The central control system sends instructions to each drone through a wireless communication channel.
4. **Coordination:** The drones coordinate their flight paths to avoid collisions and optimize delivery routes.
5. **Status Updates:** Drones periodically send status updates (e.g., battery level, current location, and task progress) to the central control system.

Step-by-Step Example: Decentralized Communication and Coordination

Scenario: A team of AI agents working on a research project.

1. **Shared Knowledge Base:** Agents share information and data through a shared knowledge base.
2. **Peer-to-Peer Communication:** Agents can communicate directly with each other to coordinate tasks and share results.
3. **Emergent Behavior:** Agents can learn from each other and adapt their strategies based on the collective intelligence of the team.

Visual Representation: A Communication Network

Single Agent	Network	Supervisor
Supervisor (as tools)	Hierarchical	Custom

Key Considerations for Effective Communication and Coordination:

- **Communication Protocols:** Use reliable and efficient communication protocols.
- **Synchronization:** Ensure that agents are synchronized to avoid conflicts and delays.
- **Conflict Resolution:** Develop strategies to resolve conflicts and disagreements between agents.
- **Scalability:** The communication and coordination mechanisms should be scalable to accommodate increasing numbers of agents.
- **Security:** Implement security measures to protect sensitive information and prevent unauthorized access.

By carefully considering these factors, we can design and implement robust and efficient CrewAI systems capable of tackling complex challenges.

Challenges and Considerations

- **Communication Delays:** Delays in communication can lead to suboptimal performance.
- **Noise and Interference:** Noise and interference can degrade the quality of communication.
- **Security and Privacy:** Sensitive information must be protected from unauthorized access.
- **Scalability:** As the number of agents increases, the complexity of communication and coordination also increases.

By carefully designing communication and coordination mechanisms, we can overcome these challenges and build robust and efficient CrewAI systems.

3.3 Task Assignment and Load Balancing

In a CrewAI system, effective task assignment and load balancing are crucial for optimal performance and efficiency.

Task Assignment Task assignment involves allocating specific tasks to suitable agents. This process can be centralized or decentralized.

- **Centralized Task Assignment:** A central controller assigns tasks to agents based on their capabilities, workload, and the current state of the system.
- **Decentralized Task Assignment:** Agents can negotiate and self-assign tasks based on their individual preferences and priorities. This approach can be more flexible and scalable, but it requires careful coordination to avoid conflicts and inefficiencies.

Load Balancing Load balancing ensures that the workload is distributed evenly among agents. This helps to prevent overloading of individual agents and maximizes system performance. Several strategies can be employed for load balancing:

- **Static Load Balancing:** Tasks are assigned to agents based on predetermined rules or policies.
- **Dynamic Load Balancing:** Agents can dynamically adjust their workload based on current conditions and the needs of the system.
- **Adaptive Load Balancing:** The system can learn from past performance and adjust the load balancing strategy to optimize performance.

Understanding the Concepts

- **Task Assignment:** The process of allocating specific tasks to suitable agents within a CrewAI system.
- **Load Balancing:** The distribution of workload among agents to ensure optimal performance and efficiency.

Real-world Analogy: A Restaurant Kitchen

Imagine a busy restaurant kitchen. The chef (central controller) assigns tasks (preparing dishes) to different kitchen staff (agents) based on their skills and the current workload. A skilled chef might be assigned to complex dishes, while a less experienced one might handle simpler tasks. The chef also monitors the workload of each staff member and reassigns tasks if needed to avoid bottlenecks.

Step-by-Step Example: Centralized Task Assignment

Scenario: A warehouse with three robots (agents) and a central control system.

1. **Task Identification:**
    - The control system identifies tasks like picking items, packing boxes, and transporting goods.
2. **Agent Capability Assessment:**
    - The control system assesses the capabilities of each robot, considering factors like battery level, carrying capacity, and speed.

3. **Task Allocation:**
    - The control system assigns tasks to robots based on their capabilities and current workload. For example:
        - Robot 1: Strong and fast, suitable for heavy lifting and long-distance transport.
        - Robot 2: Agile and precise, ideal for delicate tasks like picking small items.
        - Robot 3: Versatile, capable of handling a variety of tasks.
4. **Load Balancing:**
    - The control system monitors the workload of each robot and reassigns tasks as needed to maintain a balanced workload.
    - If one robot is overloaded, tasks can be reassigned to other robots with lower workloads.

Step-by-Step Example: Decentralized Task Assignment

Scenario: A team of AI agents working on a research project.

1. **Task Breakdown:**
    - The project is broken down into smaller tasks, such as data collection, data analysis, and report writing.
2. **Agent Negotiation:**
    - Agents negotiate with each other to assign tasks based on their expertise and preferences.
    - For example, an agent with strong data analysis skills might volunteer to lead the data analysis task.
3. **Dynamic Adjustment:**
    - As the project progresses, agents may renegotiate tasks based on changing circumstances, such as unexpected challenges or the availability of new resources.

Key Considerations for Effective Task Assignment and Load Balancing:

- **Agent Capabilities:** Consider the strengths and weaknesses of each agent.
- **Workload Distribution:** Ensure that tasks are distributed evenly to avoid overloading individual agents.

- **Communication:** Effective communication between agents is crucial for coordination and task sharing.
- **Dynamic Adaptation:** The system should be able to adapt to changing conditions and adjust task assignments accordingly.
- **Monitoring and Optimization:** Continuously monitor the system's performance and make adjustments to improve efficiency.

By carefully considering these factors, we can design and implement efficient and effective CrewAI systems.

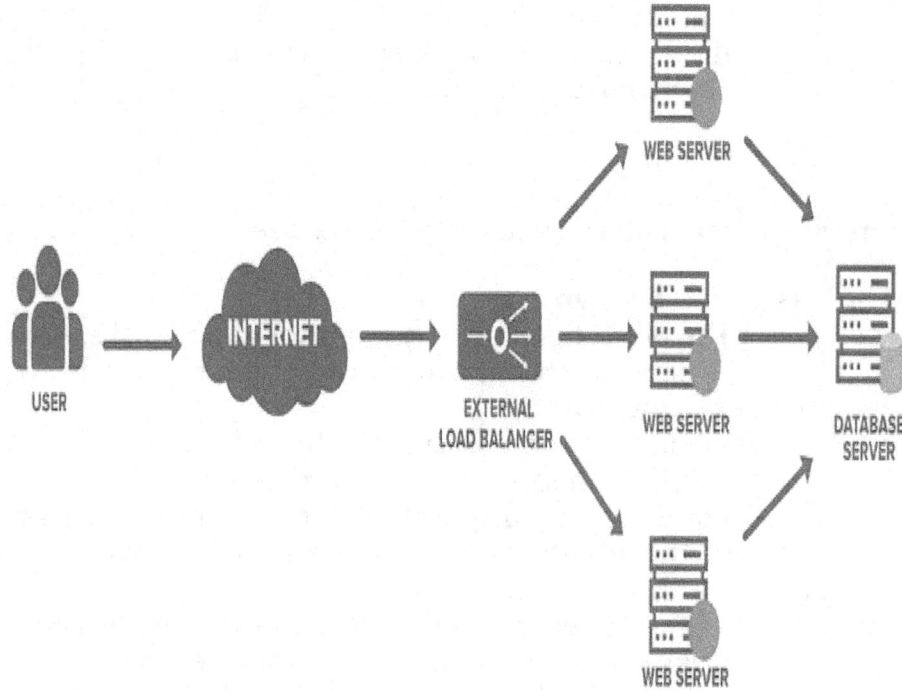

Key Considerations for Task Assignment and Load Balancing

- **Agent Capabilities:** Consider the capabilities and limitations of each agent when assigning tasks.
- **Workload Distribution:** Ensure that the workload is distributed evenly among agents to avoid overloading and underutilization.

- **Communication Overhead:** Minimize communication overhead by carefully designing task assignment and load balancing strategies.
- **Flexibility:** The system should be flexible enough to adapt to changes in the workload and agent capabilities.

By effectively assigning tasks and balancing the workload, we can optimize the performance of CrewAI systems and ensure that they can handle complex and demanding tasks.

3.4 Ethical and Security Considerations in Collaboration

As collaborative AI systems become increasingly sophisticated, it is essential to consider the ethical and security implications of their deployment.

Ethical Considerations

1. **Bias and Fairness:**
    - **Algorithmic Bias:** AI systems can inherit biases from the data they are trained on, leading to unfair and discriminatory outcomes.
    - **Mitigation Strategies:**
        - Use diverse and representative datasets.
        - Develop algorithms that are transparent and explainable.
        - Regularly audit AI systems for bias.
2. **Privacy and Data Security:**
    - **Data Protection:** Protect sensitive data from unauthorized access and misuse.
    - **Privacy-Preserving Techniques:** Implement techniques like differential privacy and federated learning to protect user privacy.
    - **Secure Communication:** Ensure secure communication channels between agents to prevent data breaches.
3. **Transparency and Accountability:**
    - **Explainable AI:** Develop AI systems that can explain their decision-making processes.

- **Human Oversight:** Implement human oversight to monitor and control AI systems.
- **Accountability Frameworks:** Establish clear accountability frameworks to address potential harms caused by AI systems.

Security Considerations

1. **Adversarial Attacks:**
   - **Adversarial Examples:** Malicious actors can manipulate input data to deceive AI systems.
   - **Defense Mechanisms:**
     - Robustness testing.
     - Adversarial training.
     - Adversarial detection.
2. **Security Breaches:**
   - **Data Breaches:** Protect sensitive data from unauthorized access.
   - **Secure Communication:** Use secure communication protocols to prevent data interception.
   - **Regular Security Audits:** Conduct regular security audits to identify and address vulnerabilities.
3. **Malicious Agents:**
   - **Agent Compromise:** Malicious actors can compromise agents and use them to disrupt the system.
   - **Detection and Response:** Develop mechanisms to detect and respond to malicious agent behavior.

By carefully considering these ethical and security issues, we can develop responsible and trustworthy collaborative AI systems. It is essential to adopt a proactive approach to addressing these challenges to ensure the safe and beneficial deployment of AI technology.

Part II
Setting Up CrewAI Systems

Chapter 4 Getting Started with CrewAI Tools

4.1 Overview of Popular CrewAI Tools and Platforms

As the field of collaborative AI continues to evolve, a variety of tools and platforms have emerged to facilitate the development and deployment of CrewAI systems. Here are some of the most popular options:

Open-Source Frameworks

- **Ray:** A popular framework for distributed computing and parallel programming. It provides tools for building and deploying large-scale machine learning applications, including collaborative AI systems.
- **Jupyter Notebook:** A versatile tool for interactive computing, data analysis, and machine learning. It's often used for prototyping and experimenting with collaborative AI algorithms.
- **TensorFlow and PyTorch:** These deep learning frameworks can be used to build individual AI agents, which can then be integrated into a collaborative AI system.

Cloud-Based Platforms

- **Google Cloud Platform (GCP):** GCP offers a range of AI and machine learning services, including AI Platform, Vertex AI, and Cloud Functions. These services can be used to build and deploy scalable collaborative AI systems.
- **Amazon Web Services (AWS):** AWS provides a comprehensive suite of cloud computing services, including SageMaker, which can be used for building, training, and deploying machine learning models.
- **Microsoft Azure:** Azure offers a variety of AI services, such as Azure Machine Learning, Azure Cognitive Services, and Azure IoT Hub. These services can be used to create

intelligent agents and connect them to form collaborative AI systems.

Specialized CrewAI Platforms

- **Unity:** A game engine that can be used to create virtual environments for training and testing AI agents. It provides a flexible platform for building and simulating collaborative AI systems.
- **RoboMaker:** A cloud-based robotics development platform that enables developers to build, test, and deploy robotic applications. It includes tools for simulation, fleet management, and AI integration.

When choosing a tool or platform, consider the following factors:

- **Scalability:** The ability to handle increasing numbers of agents and data.
- **Flexibility:** The ability to customize and extend the platform to meet specific needs.
- **Ease of Use:** The ease of learning and using the platform.
- **Community Support:** The availability of documentation, tutorials, and a supportive community.
- **Cost:** The cost of using the platform, including licensing fees and cloud computing costs.

By carefully selecting the right tools and platforms, you can accelerate the development and deployment of your CrewAI systems.

4.2 Installation and Setup Guides

Setting Up a CrewAI Development Environment

1. Choose Your Tools:

- **Python:** A popular choice for AI development.
- **Jupyter Notebook:** A great tool for interactive coding and data analysis.
- **TensorFlow or PyTorch:** Powerful deep learning frameworks for building AI models.

- **Ray:** A framework for distributed computing and parallel programming, ideal for large-scale CrewAI systems.

2. **Install Necessary Packages:**

    - **Python:** Use a package manager like pip to install required packages:

Bash

```
pip install tensorflow keras numpy pandas matplotlib scikit-learn ray
```

- **Jupyter Notebook:**

Bash

```
pip install jupyter notebook
```

3. **Set Up a Virtual Environment (Recommended):**

    - **Create a Virtual Environment:**

Bash

```
python -m venv my_env
```

- **Activate the Environment:**

Bash

```
source my_env/bin/activate   # Linux/macOS
my_env\Scripts\activate      # Windows
```

- **Install Packages:**

Bash

pip install tensorflow keras numpy pandas matplotlib scikit-learn ray

4. **Cloud-Based Platforms:**

    - **Google Cloud Platform (GCP):**
        1. Create a GCP account.
        2. Set up a project.
        3. Enable the necessary AI Platform services.
        4. Use the GCP console or the gcloud command-line tool to manage your resources.
    - **Amazon Web Services (AWS):**
        1. Create an AWS account.
        2. Set up an AWS account.
        3. Enable the necessary SageMaker services.
        4. Use the AWS Management Console or the AWS CLI to manage your resources.
    - **Microsoft Azure:**
        1. Create an Azure account.
        2. Set up an Azure subscription.
        3. Enable the necessary Azure Machine Learning services.
        4. Use the Azure portal or the Azure CLI to manage your resources.

5. **Configure Your Development Environment:**

    - **Set up a suitable development environment:** Choose a text editor or IDE like Visual Studio Code, PyCharm, or Jupyter Notebook.
    - **Configure your machine learning framework:** Follow the specific instructions for TensorFlow or PyTorch to set up the necessary configurations.
    - **Install additional libraries:** Depending on your specific requirements, you may need to install additional libraries like OpenCV for computer vision or NLTK for natural language processing.

By following these steps, you can set up a robust development environment for your CrewAI projects. Remember to consult the official documentation of your chosen tools and platforms for specific instructions and troubleshooting tips.

4.3 Choosing the Right Tools for Your Needs

When embarking on a CrewAI project, selecting the appropriate tools and platforms is crucial. The ideal choice depends on various factors, including the complexity of the project, the team's expertise, and the available resources.

Key Considerations

- **Scalability:** As your CrewAI system grows, ensure your chosen tools can handle increasing workloads and data volumes.
- **Flexibility:** The tools should be adaptable to different AI architectures and problem domains.
- **Ease of Use:** A user-friendly interface and clear documentation can significantly accelerate development.
- **Community Support:** A strong community can provide valuable resources, tutorials, and assistance.
- **Cost:** Consider the licensing costs and cloud computing expenses associated with different tools and platforms.

Popular Tool Combinations

Here are some popular tool combinations for different CrewAI projects:

For Small-Scale Projects:

- **Python:** A versatile language for general-purpose programming and AI.
- **Jupyter Notebook:** An interactive environment for data analysis and experimentation.
- **TensorFlow or PyTorch:** Powerful deep learning frameworks for building AI models.
- **Ray:** A framework for distributed computing and parallel programming.

For Large-Scale, Distributed Projects:

- **Google Cloud Platform (GCP):** Cloud-based platform for scalable machine learning and AI.
- **Amazon Web Services (AWS):** Comprehensive cloud platform with various AI and machine learning services.
- **Microsoft Azure:** Cloud platform with a range of AI and machine learning tools.

For Robotics and Simulation:

- **Unity:** A game engine for creating virtual environments and simulating AI agents.
- **ROS (Robot Operating System):** A flexible framework for building robot applications.

Tips for Tool Selection

- **Start Small:** Begin with a simple setup and gradually add complexity as your project grows.
- **Leverage Existing Tools:** Use existing tools and libraries whenever possible to accelerate development.
- **Experiment and Iterate:** Try different tools and techniques to find the best approach for your specific needs.
- **Stay Updated:** Keep up with the latest advancements in AI and machine learning tools.

By carefully considering these factors and following these tips, you can select the right tools to build effective and scalable CrewAI systems.

4.4 Basic Setup for a Collaborative AI Project

Defining the Problem and Goals

The first step in setting up a CrewAI project is to clearly define the problem you want to solve and the goals you want to achieve. This will help you determine the appropriate AI agents, their roles, and the overall system architecture.

Example:

- **Problem:** Improve customer service efficiency in an e-commerce store.
- **Goals:**
    - Reduce customer wait times.
    - Increase customer satisfaction.
    - Automate routine tasks.

Designing the AI Agents

Once you have defined the problem and goals, you can start designing the AI agents that will work together to solve the problem. Consider the following:

- **Agent Roles:** Define the specific roles and responsibilities of each agent. For example, you might have agents for:
    - Customer interaction
    - Product information retrieval
    - Order processing
    - Payment processing
- **Agent Capabilities:** Determine the skills and knowledge required for each agent.
- **Communication Protocols:** Define the communication protocols that agents will use to interact with each other.

Creating a Collaborative Environment

To enable effective collaboration between AI agents, you'll need to create a suitable environment:

- **Shared Knowledge Base:** A central repository for storing and sharing information.
- **Task Allocation Mechanism:** A system for assigning tasks to agents based on their capabilities and workload.
- **Coordination Mechanism:** A mechanism for coordinating the actions of multiple agents, such as a centralized controller or decentralized coordination.

Implementing the System

1. **Choose a Framework:** Select a suitable framework or platform to build your CrewAI system. Consider factors like scalability, flexibility, and ease of use.
2. **Develop AI Agents:** Implement the AI agents using appropriate algorithms and techniques, such as machine learning, natural language processing, or computer vision.
3. **Integrate Agents:** Connect the agents and configure their communication and coordination mechanisms.
4. **Test and Deploy:** Thoroughly test the system to ensure it works as expected. Deploy the system to a production environment and monitor its performance.

Example: A Collaborative AI System for E-commerce

- **Agent 1: Customer Interaction Agent:** Uses natural language processing to understand customer queries and provide relevant information.
- **Agent 2: Product Information Agent:** Retrieves product information from a database and provides it to the customer interaction agent.
- **Agent 3: Order Processing Agent:** Processes orders, calculates shipping costs, and updates inventory.
- **Agent 4: Payment Processing Agent:** Handles payment transactions and generates invoices.

These agents collaborate to provide efficient and accurate customer service. The customer interaction agent handles initial customer inquiries, while the other agents work behind the scenes to fulfill requests and process orders.

Chapter 5 Building Your First CrewAI Workflow

5.1 Defining Goals and Requirements

Before embarking on any CrewAI project, it's crucial to clearly define your goals and requirements. This will guide the development process and ensure that the final system aligns with your objectives.

Key Steps in Goal and Requirement Definition

1. **Identify the Problem:**
    - Clearly articulate the problem you want to solve. What are the specific challenges or inefficiencies that you aim to address?
    - For example, you might want to improve customer service response times, optimize supply chain logistics, or accelerate drug discovery.
2. **Define the Goals:**
    - Set specific, measurable, achievable, relevant, and time-bound (SMART) goals.
    - Break down broad goals into smaller, more manageable sub-goals.
    - For instance, a goal might be to reduce customer wait times by 20% within six months.
3. **Identify the Key Tasks:**
    - Determine the core tasks that need to be performed to achieve your goals.
    - Break down complex tasks into smaller, more manageable subtasks.
4. **Determine the Required AI Capabilities:**
    - Identify the specific AI techniques and algorithms that will be needed to accomplish the tasks.
    - Consider factors such as machine learning, natural language processing, computer vision, and reinforcement learning.
5. **Define the Data Requirements:**

- Identify the types of data that will be required to train and operate the AI agents.
- Consider the data sources, data quality, and data privacy requirements.

Example: A Collaborative AI System for Healthcare

- **Problem:** Improve patient diagnosis and treatment.
- **Goals:**
    - Increase diagnostic accuracy.
    - Reduce treatment time.
    - Improve patient outcomes.
- **Key Tasks:**
    - Analyze medical images.
    - Process patient records.
    - Predict disease progression.
    - Recommend treatment plans.
- **Required AI Capabilities:**
    - Computer vision for image analysis.
    - Natural language processing for processing medical reports.
    - Machine learning for predictive modeling.

By carefully defining your goals and requirements, you can lay a strong foundation for your CrewAI project and ensure that it delivers the desired outcomes.

5.2 Creating a Simple Task Flow

Once you've defined your goals and requirements, the next step is to create a simple task flow for your CrewAI system. This involves breaking down the overall task into smaller, more manageable subtasks and assigning them to specific AI agents.

Here's a general approach to creating a task flow:

1. **Identify the Main Task:**
    - Clearly define the primary task that your CrewAI system needs to accomplish.
    - For example, in a customer service chatbot, the main task might be to answer customer queries.

2. **Break Down the Task:**
    - Divide the main task into smaller, more specific subtasks.
    - For instance, the "answer customer query" task can be broken down into:
        - Understand the query
        - Retrieve relevant information
        - Generate a response
        - Deliver the response
3. **Assign Tasks to Agents:**
    - Assign each subtask to a specific AI agent based on its capabilities and expertise.
    - For example, a natural language processing agent can handle understanding the query and generating a response, while a knowledge base agent can retrieve relevant information.
4. **Define the Sequence of Tasks:**
    - Determine the order in which the tasks should be executed.
    - Consider any dependencies between tasks and ensure that they are executed in the correct sequence.
5. **Visualize the Task Flow:**
    - Use a flowchart or a diagram to visually represent the task flow.
    - This can help you identify potential bottlenecks and inefficiencies.

Example: Task Flow for a Customer Service Chatbot

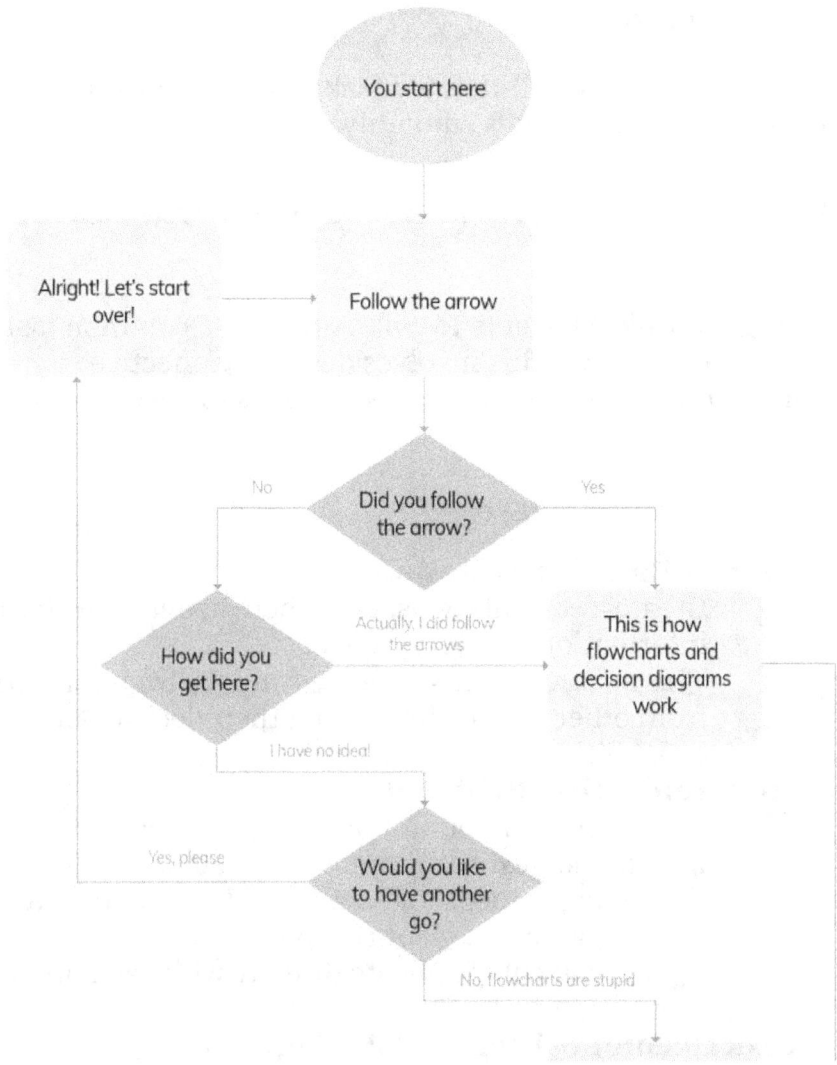

Key Considerations:

- **Task Dependencies:** Identify any dependencies between tasks and ensure that they are executed in the correct order.
- **Error Handling:** Consider potential errors or exceptions and implement appropriate error handling mechanisms.
- **Flexibility:** Design the task flow to be flexible and adaptable to changing circumstances.

- **Performance Optimization:** Identify opportunities to optimize the task flow to improve efficiency and reduce processing time.

By creating a clear and well-defined task flow, you can ensure that your CrewAI system operates smoothly and efficiently.

5.3 Integrating Multiple AI Agents for a Common Task

Integrating multiple AI agents to collaborate on a common task is a core aspect of CrewAI. This involves designing effective communication and coordination mechanisms to ensure seamless collaboration.

Key Strategies for Integration:

1. **Shared Knowledge Base:**
   - Create a central repository where agents can share information and knowledge.
   - This enables agents to access and utilize information from other agents, improving their decision-making capabilities.
2. **Communication Protocols:**
   - Establish clear communication protocols to facilitate information exchange between agents.
   - Common protocols like REST API, gRPC, or message queues can be used for this purpose.
   - Agents can communicate directly with each other or through a central hub.
3. **Task Decomposition and Assignment:**
   - Break down complex tasks into smaller, more manageable subtasks.
   - Assign subtasks to appropriate agents based on their capabilities and workload.
   - Use task allocation algorithms to optimize resource utilization.
4. **Coordination and Synchronization:**
   - Implement mechanisms to coordinate the actions of multiple agents.

- Use techniques like time synchronization, shared clocks, or centralized planning.
- Consider using a shared blackboard or white board to coordinate shared information and knowledge.
5. **Conflict Resolution:**
    - Develop strategies to handle conflicts that may arise between agents, such as competing for resources or having different opinions.
    - Implement negotiation mechanisms or arbitration processes to resolve conflicts.

Example: A Collaborative AI System for Medical Diagnosis

- **Image Analysis Agent:** Analyzes medical images (X-rays, CT scans, MRIs) to identify abnormalities.
- **Natural Language Processing Agent:** Processes patient records and medical literature to extract relevant information.
- **Knowledge Base Agent:** Stores and retrieves medical knowledge and guidelines.

These agents collaborate to diagnose a patient's condition:

1. **Image Analysis Agent** analyzes the medical images and identifies potential abnormalities.
2. **Natural Language Processing Agent** extracts relevant information from patient records and medical literature.
3. **Knowledge Base Agent** provides medical guidelines and best practices.
4. The agents share information and collaborate to reach a diagnosis.

Understanding the Concept

In a CrewAI system, multiple AI agents can collaborate to solve complex problems. This often involves breaking down a complex task into smaller, more manageable subtasks and assigning them to different agents. The agents then work together to achieve the overall goal.

A Real-World Example: Autonomous Vehicle

Task: Navigate a busy intersection safely.

Agents:

1. **Perception Agent:** Detects objects (cars, pedestrians, traffic lights) using sensors like cameras and LiDAR.
2. **Prediction Agent:** Predicts the future movement of objects based on their current state and historical data.
3. **Planning Agent:** Plans the vehicle's trajectory to reach its destination safely and efficiently.
4. **Control Agent:** Executes the planned trajectory by sending commands to the vehicle's actuators.

Collaboration:

1. **Perception Agent** sends detected objects and their properties to the **Prediction Agent**.
2. **Prediction Agent** predicts the future trajectories of objects and sends the predictions to the **Planning Agent**.
3. **Planning Agent** generates a safe and efficient trajectory and sends it to the **Control Agent**.
4. **Control Agent** executes the trajectory by controlling the vehicle's steering, acceleration, and braking.

A Code Example: A Collaborative AI System for Image Captioning

Task: Generate descriptive captions for images.

Agents:

1. **Feature Extraction Agent:** Extracts visual features from the image using a pre-trained convolutional neural network (CNN).

2. **Caption Generation Agent:** Generates captions using a recurrent neural network (RNN) based on the extracted features.
3. **Language Model Agent:** Refines the captions using a language model to improve grammar and coherence.

Code Implementation:

Python

```python
import torch
import torchvision.models as models
import torch.nn as nn
import nltk


# Feature Extraction Agent
class FeatureExtractor(nn.Module):
    def __init__(self):
        super(FeatureExtractor, self).__init__()
        self.resnet = models.resnet50(pretrained=True)
        for param in self.resnet.parameters():
            param.requires_grad = False

    def forward(self, x):
        x = self.resnet(x)
        return x
```

```python
# Caption Generation Agent

class CaptionGenerator(nn.Module):

    def __init__(self, vocab_size, embed_dim, hidden_dim, num_layers):

        super(CaptionGenerator, self).__init__()

        self.embed = nn.Embedding(vocab_size, embed_dim)

        self.lstm = nn.LSTM(embed_dim, hidden_dim, num_layers)

        self.linear = nn.Linear(hidden_dim, vocab_size)


    def forward(self, features, caption_length):

        # ... (implementation details)

        return captions


# Language Model Agent

class LanguageModelAgent(nn.Module):

    def __init__(self, vocab_size, embed_dim, hidden_dim, num_layers):

        super(LanguageModelAgent, self).__init__()

        # ... (implementation details)
```

```python
    def forward(self, text):
        # ... (implementation details)
        return refined_text


# Main Function
def main():
    # ... (load models, preprocess image, etc.)
    features = feature_extractor(image)
    caption = caption_generator(features)
    refined_caption = language_model_agent(caption)
    print(refined_caption)
```

Key Considerations for Effective Integration:

- **Clear Communication Channels:** Ensure that agents can effectively communicate and share information.
- **Task Decomposition:** Break down complex tasks into smaller, manageable subtasks.
- **Synchronization:** Coordinate the actions of agents to avoid conflicts and inefficiencies.
- **Error Handling:** Implement robust error handling mechanisms to deal with unexpected situations.
- **Continuous Learning:** Enable agents to learn from each other and improve their performance over time.

By integrating multiple AI agents, we can create more powerful and intelligent systems capable of solving complex problems. Effective integration requires careful planning, design, and implementation.

5.4 Hands-On Example: A Basic CrewAI Project

Problem: Build a simple CrewAI system to classify images into two categories: "cat" and "dog".

Agents:

1. **Image Preprocessing Agent:** Prepares images for input to the neural network.
2. **Feature Extraction Agent:** Extracts features from the preprocessed images.
3. **Classification Agent:** Classifies the images based on the extracted features.

Task Flow:

1. **Image Preprocessing:**
   - Resize images to a standard size.
   - Convert images to a suitable format (e.g., RGB).
   - Normalize pixel values.
2. **Feature Extraction:**
   - Use a pre-trained convolutional neural network (CNN) to extract high-level features.
3. **Classification:**
   - Feed the extracted features into a classifier (e.g., a fully connected neural network) to predict the image class.

Code Implementation:

Python

```python
import torch

import torchvision.models as models

import torchvision.transforms as transforms
```

```python
# Image Preprocessing Agent
class ImagePreprocessor:
    def __init__(self):
        self.transform = transforms.Compose([
            transforms.Resize(256),
            transforms.CenterCrop(224),
            transforms.ToTensor(),
            transforms.Normalize(mean=[0.485, 0.456, 0.406], std=[0.229, 0.224, 0.225])
        ])

    def preprocess(self, image_path):
        image = Image.open(image_path)
        image_tensor = self.transform(image).unsqueeze(0)
        return image_tensor


# Feature Extraction Agent
class FeatureExtractor:
    def __init__(self):
        self.model = models.resnet50(pretrained=True)
        for param in self.model.parameters():
```

```python
            param.requires_grad = False

    def extract_features(self, image_tensor):
        with torch.no_grad():
            features = self.model(image_tensor)
        return features


# Classification Agent
class Classifier:
    def __init__(self, num_classes):
        self.model = nn.Sequential(
            nn.Linear(1000, 512),
            nn.ReLU(),
            nn.Dropout(0.5),
            nn.Linear(512, num_classes)
        )

    def forward(self, features):
        logits = self.model(features)
        return logits


# Main Function
```

```python
def main():
    # ... (load models, preprocess image, etc.)
    preprocessed_image = image_preprocessor.preprocess(image_path)
    features = feature_extractor.extract_features(preprocessed_image)
    logits = classifier(features)
    _, predicted_class = torch.max(logits, 1)
    print("Predicted class:", predicted_class)
```

Key Points:

- **Clear Task Division:** Each agent is responsible for a specific task, making the system modular and easier to maintain.
- **Efficient Communication:** The agents communicate through data sharing, ensuring smooth information flow.
- **Scalability:** The system can be easily scaled by adding more agents or increasing the complexity of existing agents.
- **Flexibility:** The system can be adapted to different tasks and domains by modifying the agents and their interactions.

By following these steps and considering the key principles of CrewAI, you can build effective and efficient collaborative AI systems.

Chapter 6 Configuring Communication and Task Coordination

6.1 How AI Agents Communicate and Collaborate

Effective communication and coordination are crucial for successful collaboration among AI agents. These mechanisms allow agents to share information, synchronize their actions, and collectively solve complex problems.

Communication Protocols

AI agents can communicate through various protocols, including:

- **Message Passing:** Agents exchange messages directly, either synchronously or asynchronously. This is a common approach for point-to-point communication.
- **Shared Memory:** Agents access and modify a shared memory space. This is efficient for frequent data sharing between agents.
- **Blackboard Architecture:** Agents write information to and read information from a shared blackboard. This is useful for coordinating complex tasks and sharing intermediate results.
- **Publish-Subscribe:** Agents publish messages to specific topics, and other agents subscribe to those topics to receive relevant information.

Coordination Mechanisms

Several coordination mechanisms can be used to ensure that AI agents work together effectively:

- **Centralized Control:** A central controller coordinates the activities of all agents. This approach is suitable for simple systems, but it can become a bottleneck as the number of agents increases.

- **Decentralized Control:** Agents coordinate their actions without a central controller. This approach is more scalable and robust, but it requires careful design and implementation.
- **Hybrid Approach:** A combination of centralized and decentralized control can be used to balance the advantages of both approaches.

Key Considerations for Effective Communication and Coordination

- **Communication Efficiency:** Minimize communication overhead to improve performance.
- **Synchronization:** Ensure that agents are synchronized to avoid conflicts and inconsistencies.
- **Error Handling:** Implement mechanisms to handle communication failures and errors.
- **Security:** Protect sensitive information and prevent unauthorized access.
- **Scalability:** Design the communication and coordination mechanisms to handle increasing numbers of agents.

By carefully designing communication and coordination mechanisms, we can create robust and efficient CrewAI systems.

6.2 Setting Up Messaging Protocols

Understanding the Need

In a CrewAI system, effective communication between agents is crucial. Messaging protocols provide a standardized way for agents to exchange information.

Popular Messaging Protocols for AI

1. **Message Queues:**
    - **RabbitMQ:** A powerful and flexible message broker that supports various messaging patterns.
    - **Kafka:** A high-throughput, distributed streaming platform.
2. **RESTful APIs:**

- A versatile approach for building web services that can be used for agent-to-agent communication.
3. **gRPC:**
    - A modern, high-performance RPC framework that uses protocol buffers for efficient data serialization.

Key Considerations for Setting Up Messaging Protocols

1. **Reliability:**
    - Ensure reliable message delivery, even in case of network failures or system crashes.
    - Implement mechanisms like message acknowledgment and retries.
2. **Scalability:**
    - Choose a protocol that can handle increasing numbers of agents and message traffic.
    - Consider using distributed messaging systems like Kafka.
3. **Security:**
    - Protect sensitive information by using encryption and authentication mechanisms.
    - Implement access controls to restrict access to authorized agents.
4. **Latency:**
    - Minimize latency to ensure timely communication and coordination between agents.
    - Consider using low-latency protocols like gRPC.
5. **Error Handling:**
    - Implement robust error handling mechanisms to deal with message loss, network failures, and other issues.

Example: A Simple Message Queue-Based Communication

Let's consider a scenario where two agents, Agent A and Agent B, need to communicate. Agent A sends a task to Agent B, and Agent B processes the task and sends the result back to Agent A.

1. **Set up a Message Queue:**
    - Install a message queue system like RabbitMQ.

        ○ Configure the broker and create the necessary queues and exchanges.
    2. **Agent A:**
        ○ Enqueue a task message to a specific queue.
    3. **Agent B:**
        ○ Consumes messages from the queue.
        ○ Processes the task.
        ○ Enqueues the result to another queue.
    4. **Agent A:**
        ○ Consumes the result message from the second queue.

Code Example (Simplified):

Python

```
import pika


# Agent A
def send_task(connection, channel, queue_name, task):
    channel.basic_publish(exchange='', routing_key=queue_name, body=task)


# Agent B
def consume_task(connection, channel, queue_name):
    def callback(ch, method, properties, body):
        # Process the task
        result = process_task(body)
        # Send the result back to Agent A
```

```
        send_result(connection, channel,
'result_queue', result)


    channel.basic_consume(queue=queue_name,
on_message_callback=callback, auto_ack=True)

    channel.start_consuming()
```

By carefully selecting and configuring messaging protocols, we can ensure effective communication and coordination between AI agents in a CrewAI system.

6.3 Task Distribution Strategies

Effective task distribution is crucial for optimizing the performance of a CrewAI system. It involves assigning tasks to agents based on their capabilities, workload, and the overall system goals.

Key Task Distribution Strategies:

1. **Centralized Task Allocation:**
    - A central controller assigns tasks to agents based on their capabilities and current workload.
    - **Advantages:** Ensures efficient resource utilization and avoids conflicts.
    - **Disadvantages:** Can become a bottleneck, especially in large-scale systems.
2. **Decentralized Task Allocation:**
    - Agents negotiate and self-assign tasks based on their individual capabilities and preferences.
    - **Advantages:** More flexible and scalable.
    - **Disadvantages:** Can lead to suboptimal task assignments and potential conflicts.
3. **Hybrid Task Allocation:**
    - Combines centralized and decentralized approaches.

- A central controller may assign high-level tasks, while agents negotiate and self-assign subtasks.
- **Advantages:** Balances the benefits of centralized and decentralized approaches.

Factors to Consider for Task Distribution:

- **Agent Capabilities:** Consider the strengths and weaknesses of each agent.
- **Workload Balancing:** Distribute tasks evenly to avoid overloading individual agents.
- **Communication Overhead:** Minimize communication overhead by optimizing task assignments.
- **Dynamic Adaptation:** The system should be able to adapt to changes in the workload and agent capabilities.
- **Error Handling:** Implement mechanisms to handle task failures and reassign tasks if necessary.

Example: Task Distribution in a Collaborative Robotics System

Consider a collaborative robotics system consisting of two robots: Robot A and Robot B. The task is to assemble a product.

- **Centralized Task Allocation:** A central controller assigns specific tasks to each robot, such as assembling the base, attaching the components, and performing quality checks.
- **Decentralized Task Allocation:** Robots negotiate and self-assign tasks based on their current positions, battery levels, and task priorities. For example, Robot A might take on a task closer to its current position, while Robot B might handle a more complex task that requires specialized tools.

By carefully considering these factors and employing appropriate task distribution strategies, we can optimize the performance and efficiency of CrewAI systems.

6.4 Examples of Communication Models in Action

Let's explore some real-world examples of communication models used in CrewAI systems.

1. Collaborative Filtering

- **Agents:** Multiple users.
- **Communication Model:** Implicit communication through user ratings and preferences.
- **How it Works:** Users rate items (e.g., movies, products) on a platform. The system analyzes these ratings to identify similarities between users and items. By understanding these relationships, the system can recommend items to users that they might like.

2. Multi-Agent Reinforcement Learning

- **Agents:** Multiple AI agents.
- **Communication Model:** Explicit communication through shared rewards and observations.
- **How it Works:** Agents learn to collaborate by observing the environment, taking actions, and receiving rewards or penalties. They can communicate with each other to share information and coordinate their actions.

3. Distributed Machine Learning

- **Agents:** Multiple machines or nodes.
- **Communication Model:** Explicit communication through a parameter server.
- **How it Works:** The parameter server stores and updates model parameters. Worker nodes request and update parameters from the server, and then train their local models. The updated models are then sent back to the parameter server.

4. Swarm Intelligence

- **Agents:** Multiple simple agents.

- **Communication Model:** Implicit communication through local interactions.
- **How it Works:** Agents interact with their environment and each other to collectively solve problems. For example, ants can find the shortest path to a food source through a process of trial and error and pheromone trails.

Key Considerations for Effective Communication Models

- **Efficiency:** Minimize communication overhead to improve performance.
- **Scalability:** The communication model should be able to handle increasing numbers of agents.
- **Robustness:** The system should be resilient to failures and disruptions.
- **Security:** Protect sensitive information and prevent unauthorized access.
- **Privacy:** Ensure that user privacy is protected.

By carefully designing and implementing communication models, we can create powerful and effective CrewAI systems.

Chapter 7 Data Sharing and Processing in CrewAI

7.1 Understanding Data Flow and Sharing

Data Flow in CrewAI Systems

In a CrewAI system, data flows between different agents to enable collaboration and decision-making. Understanding the data flow is crucial for efficient and effective operation.

Key Components of Data Flow:

- **Data Sources:** These can be various sources like sensors, databases, or APIs.
- **Data Preprocessing:** Raw data is cleaned, transformed, and prepared for analysis.
- **Data Sharing:** Data is shared among agents through communication channels.
- **Data Storage:** Data is stored in databases or data warehouses for future reference.
- **Data Visualization:** Data is visualized to gain insights and make informed decisions.

Data Sharing Mechanisms:

- **Shared Memory:** Agents access and modify a shared memory space. This is efficient for frequent data sharing between agents.
- **Message Passing:** Agents exchange data through messages. This is suitable for asynchronous communication and data sharing between distant agents.
- **Distributed File Systems:** Agents can access and modify files stored in a distributed file system. This is useful for sharing large datasets.
- **Data Lakes and Data Warehouses:** Centralized repositories for storing and managing large volumes of data.

Challenges in Data Sharing:

- **Data Quality:** Ensuring data accuracy, completeness, and consistency.
- **Data Privacy:** Protecting sensitive data from unauthorized access.
- **Data Security:** Implementing measures to prevent data breaches and cyberattacks.
- **Data Compatibility:** Ensuring that data from different sources can be integrated and processed.
- **Data Latency:** Minimizing data transfer delays to ensure timely decision-making.

By understanding the data flow and implementing effective data sharing mechanisms, we can build robust and efficient CrewAI systems.

7.2 Data Integration and Compatibility Issues

Data Integration

Data integration is the process of combining data from multiple sources into a unified view. In CrewAI systems, data integration is crucial for enabling collaboration between agents.

Key Challenges in Data Integration:

- **Data Heterogeneity:** Data from different sources may have different formats, structures, and quality.
- **Data Quality Issues:** Data may contain errors, inconsistencies, or missing values.
- **Data Security and Privacy:** Sensitive data must be protected from unauthorized access.
- **Data Latency:** Delays in data transfer can impact the performance of the system.

Strategies for Data Integration:

- **Data Cleaning and Preprocessing:**
  - Handle missing values, outliers, and inconsistencies.
  - Normalize and standardize data.

- **Data Transformation:**
  - Convert data into a common format.
  - Aggregate or disaggregate data as needed.
- **Data Integration Techniques:**
  - **ETL (Extract, Transform, Load):** Extract data from source systems, transform it into a suitable format, and load it into a target system.
  - **Data Federation:** Create a virtual view of data from multiple sources without physically integrating it.
  - **Data Virtualization:** Create a layer of abstraction over data sources to provide a unified view.

Data Compatibility Issues

Data compatibility refers to the ability of different data sources to work together seamlessly. Common compatibility issues include:

- **Data Formats:** Different data formats (e.g., CSV, JSON, XML) may require conversion.
- **Data Schemas:** Inconsistent data schemas can hinder data integration.
- **Data Quality:** Differences in data quality can impact the accuracy of analysis and decision-making.

Strategies for Addressing Data Compatibility Issues:

- **Data Standardization:** Define common data standards and formats.
- **Data Mapping:** Map data elements from different sources to a common schema.
- **Data Cleaning and Preprocessing:** Clean and preprocess data to ensure consistency and quality.
- **Data Quality Assurance:** Implement data quality checks and monitoring.

By effectively addressing data integration and compatibility issues, we can ensure the smooth operation of CrewAI systems.

7.3 Best Practices for Secure Data Handling

In a CrewAI system, data security is paramount. Protecting sensitive data from unauthorized access, breaches, and misuse is crucial. Here are some best practices for secure data handling:

Data Encryption

- **Encryption at Rest:** Encrypt data stored on disk or in databases.
- **Encryption in Transit:** Encrypt data transmitted over networks.
- **Key Management:** Implement robust key management practices to protect encryption keys.

Access Control

- **Role-Based Access Control (RBAC):** Grant access to data based on user roles and privileges.
- **Least Privilege Principle:** Grant users only the minimum necessary permissions.
- **Regular Access Reviews:** Periodically review and update access controls.

Data Privacy

- **Anonymization and Pseudonymization:** Remove personally identifiable information from data.
- **Privacy-Preserving Techniques:** Use techniques like differential privacy and federated learning to protect privacy.
- **Compliance with Data Protection Regulations:** Adhere to regulations like GDPR and CCPA.

Data Integrity

- **Data Validation:** Implement validation rules to ensure data accuracy and consistency.
- **Data Backup and Recovery:** Maintain regular backups and have a disaster recovery plan.

- **Data Monitoring:** Monitor data for anomalies and potential security threats.

Network Security

- **Secure Network Protocols:** Use secure protocols like HTTPS and SSH.
- **Firewall Protection:** Implement firewalls to protect the system from unauthorized access.
- **Intrusion Detection and Prevention Systems (IDS/IPS):** Monitor network traffic for malicious activity.

User Authentication and Authorization

- **Strong Password Policies:** Enforce strong password policies.
- **Multi-Factor Authentication (MFA):** Require multiple forms of authentication.
- **Regular Security Awareness Training:** Educate users about security best practices.

Incident Response Planning

- **Incident Response Team:** Establish a dedicated team to respond to security incidents.
- **Incident Response Plan:** Develop a plan for responding to security breaches.
- **Regular Security Audits:** Conduct regular security audits to identify vulnerabilities.

By following these best practices, you can protect your CrewAI system and the sensitive data it processes.

7.4 Examples of Data Sharing Mechanisms

In CrewAI systems, effective data sharing is essential for collaboration and decision-making. Here are some common data sharing mechanisms:

1. Shared Memory

- **How it works:** Agents access and modify a shared memory space.
- **Advantages:** Efficient for frequent data exchange between agents.
- **Disadvantages:** Can be challenging to implement in distributed systems.

Example: In a self-driving car, multiple AI agents (perception, planning, control) can share sensor data and predictions through shared memory.

2. Message Passing

- **How it works:** Agents exchange data through messages, either synchronously or asynchronously.
- **Advantages:** Flexible and suitable for distributed systems.
- **Disadvantages:** Can introduce latency and overhead.

Example: In a distributed machine learning system, worker nodes can send intermediate results and model updates to a central parameter server using message passing.

3. Distributed File Systems

- **How it works:** Agents access and modify files stored in a distributed file system.
- **Advantages:** Suitable for sharing large datasets.
- **Disadvantages:** Can be complex to implement and manage.

Example: In a scientific research project, researchers can share large datasets and analysis results using a distributed file system like Hadoop Distributed File System (HDFS).

4. Data Lakes and Data Warehouses

- **How it works:** Centralized repositories for storing and managing large volumes of data.
- **Advantages:** Provide a single source of truth for data analysis and reporting.
- **Disadvantages:** Can be complex to set up and maintain.

Example: In a retail analytics system, data from various sources (e.g., point-of-sale systems, customer relationship management systems) can be stored in a data warehouse for analysis and reporting.

5. Data Streaming

- **How it works:** Data is continuously streamed from sources to consumers.
- **Advantages:** Real-time processing and analysis of data.
- **Disadvantages:** Requires robust infrastructure and efficient data processing techniques.

Example: In a stock trading system, real-time market data can be streamed to AI agents for analysis and decision-making.

By understanding these data sharing mechanisms, you can effectively design and implement CrewAI systems that can efficiently share and process data to achieve their goals.

Part III
Core Techniques for Collaborative AI

Chapter 8: Agent Role Specialization

8.1 What is Role Specialization in CrewAI?

Role specialization in CrewAI refers to the practice of assigning specific roles and responsibilities to different AI agents within a collaborative system. By specializing agents, we can enhance their capabilities and efficiency in performing specific tasks.

Benefits of Role Specialization

- **Improved Performance:** Specialized agents can be optimized for specific tasks, leading to better performance and accuracy.
- **Efficient Resource Utilization:** Agents can focus on their core competencies, reducing redundancy and increasing overall system efficiency.
- **Scalability:** The system can be scaled by adding or removing specialized agents as needed.
- **Flexibility:** The system can adapt to changing requirements by reconfiguring or re-training specialized agents.

Example: A Collaborative AI System for Medical Diagnosis

- **Image Analysis Agent:** Specialized in analyzing medical images (X-rays, CT scans, MRIs).
- **Natural Language Processing Agent:** Specialized in processing patient records and medical literature.
- **Knowledge Base Agent:** Specialized in storing and retrieving medical knowledge and guidelines.

By assigning specific roles to each agent, the system can more effectively diagnose diseases and recommend treatment plans.

8.2 Setting Up Specialized Agents for Different Tasks

Setting up specialized AI agents involves a careful consideration of their roles, capabilities, and the overall system architecture. Here's a step-by-step approach to setting up specialized agents:

1. Identify the Required Tasks:

- Break down the complex task into smaller, more manageable subtasks.
- Analyze the specific skills and knowledge required for each subtask.

2. Design Agent Architectures:

- **Choose appropriate architectures:** Select neural network architectures (e.g., CNN, RNN, Transformer) that are suitable for the specific task.
- **Customize models:** Tailor the models to the specific requirements of the task.
- **Pre-train models:** Leverage pre-trained models to accelerate training and improve performance.

3. Train and Fine-tune Agents:

- **Collect and prepare data:** Gather relevant data for training the agents.
- **Train models:** Use appropriate training techniques (e.g., supervised learning, reinforcement learning) to train the agents.
- **Fine-tune models:** Adjust model parameters to optimize performance on specific tasks.

4. Implement Communication and Coordination Mechanisms:

- **Define communication protocols:** Establish clear communication channels between agents.
- **Implement coordination strategies:** Use techniques like task allocation, synchronization, and conflict resolution.

Example: A Collaborative AI System for Autonomous Vehicles

- **Perception Agent:** Specialized in detecting objects (cars, pedestrians, traffic signs) using sensor data.
- **Prediction Agent:** Specialized in predicting the future movement of objects.
- **Planning Agent:** Specialized in generating safe and efficient driving plans.
- **Control Agent:** Specialized in executing the driving plan by controlling the vehicle's actuators.

Key Considerations:

- **Modularity:** Design agents as modular components that can be easily replaced or modified.
- **Flexibility:** Allow for dynamic reconfiguration of agent roles and responsibilities.
- **Robustness:** Implement error handling and fault tolerance mechanisms.
- **Scalability:** Design the system to handle increasing numbers of agents and tasks.

By carefully designing and training specialized agents, we can create powerful and efficient CrewAI systems that can tackle complex problems.

8.3 Balancing Flexibility and Specialization

While specialization can significantly improve the performance of AI agents, it's important to balance specialization with flexibility. A purely specialized agent might be highly efficient at a specific task but may struggle with adapting to new or unexpected situations.

Key Strategies for Balancing Flexibility and Specialization:

1. **Multi-Task Learning:**
   - Train agents on multiple related tasks simultaneously.

- This can improve the agent's ability to generalize and adapt to new situations.
2. **Transfer Learning:**
    - Leverage pre-trained models to accelerate training and improve performance on new tasks.
    - By transferring knowledge from one task to another, agents can quickly adapt to new scenarios.
3. **Meta-Learning:**
    - Train agents to learn how to learn.
    - Meta-learning enables agents to quickly adapt to new tasks and environments.
4. **Modular Design:**
    - Design agents as modular components that can be easily combined and reconfigured.
    - This allows for flexibility in task allocation and system adaptation.
5. **Hierarchical Structures:**
    - Create hierarchical structures of agents, where higher-level agents coordinate the activities of lower-level agents.
    - This allows for both specialization and flexibility, as higher-level agents can oversee the overall system and make strategic decisions.

Example: A Collaborative AI System for Robotics

- **Specialized Agents:**
    - **Perception Agent:** Specialized in object detection and tracking.
    - **Motion Planning Agent:** Specialized in generating motion plans.
    - **Control Agent:** Specialized in executing low-level motor commands.
- **Flexibility:**
    - The system can adapt to new environments and tasks by retraining or reconfiguring the agents.
    - The agents can collaborate to solve complex tasks that require a combination of skills.

By carefully balancing specialization and flexibility, we can create robust and adaptable CrewAI systems that can excel in a variety of tasks and environments.

8.4 Real-World Examples of Role Specialization

1. Autonomous Vehicles

- **Perception Agent:** Specializes in detecting objects (pedestrians, cars, traffic signs) using sensors like cameras and LiDAR.
- **Prediction Agent:** Specializes in predicting the future movement of objects.
- **Planning Agent:** Specializes in generating safe and efficient driving plans.
- **Control Agent:** Specializes in executing the driving plan by controlling the vehicle's actuators.

2. Healthcare

- **Image Analysis Agent:** Specializes in analyzing medical images (X-rays, CT scans, MRIs) to detect anomalies.
- **Natural Language Processing Agent:** Specializes in processing medical records and literature to extract relevant information.
- **Knowledge Base Agent:** Specializes in storing and retrieving medical knowledge and guidelines.

3. Customer Service

- **Natural Language Processing Agent:** Specializes in understanding and responding to customer queries.
- **Knowledge Base Agent:** Specializes in retrieving relevant information from a knowledge base.
- **Task Completion Agent:** Specializes in performing specific tasks, such as processing orders or scheduling appointments.

4. Financial Services

- **Fraud Detection Agent:** Specializes in identifying fraudulent transactions.
- **Risk Assessment Agent:** Specializes in assessing financial risks.
- **Investment Recommendation Agent:** Specializes in providing investment advice.

By specializing agents, we can create more efficient and effective AI systems that can handle complex tasks and adapt to changing environments.

Chapter 9 Workflow Management in CrewAI Systems

9.1 Principles of Effective Workflow Management

Effective workflow management is crucial for the success of any CrewAI system. It ensures that tasks are assigned and executed efficiently, bottlenecks are minimized, and the overall system performance is optimized.

Key Principles of Effective Workflow Management:

1. **Clear Task Definition:**
    - Break down complex tasks into smaller, well-defined subtasks.
    - Clearly specify the inputs, outputs, and expected outcomes for each subtask.
2. **Task Prioritization:**
    - Prioritize tasks based on their importance and urgency.
    - Consider factors like deadlines, resource constraints, and potential impact.
3. **Agent Assignment:**
    - Assign tasks to agents based on their capabilities, workload, and availability.
    - Use intelligent task allocation algorithms to optimize resource utilization.
4. **Communication and Coordination:**
    - Establish effective communication channels between agents.
    - Implement mechanisms for coordination and synchronization.
5. **Monitoring and Control:**
    - Monitor the progress of tasks and the performance of agents.
    - Identify and address any issues or bottlenecks.
6. **Flexibility and Adaptability:**

- Design the workflow to be flexible and adaptable to changing conditions.
- Allow for dynamic reassignment of tasks and adjustment of priorities.

7. **Error Handling and Recovery:**
   - Implement robust error handling mechanisms to recover from failures and minimize disruptions.
   - Develop contingency plans for unexpected situations.

By adhering to these principles, we can create efficient and resilient CrewAI systems that can deliver high-quality results.

9.2 Monitoring Task Progress and Agent Performance

Monitoring task progress and agent performance is essential for ensuring the efficient and effective operation of a CrewAI system. It allows us to identify potential bottlenecks, optimize resource allocation, and improve overall system performance.

Key Metrics for Monitoring Task Progress:

- **Task Completion Time:** The time taken to complete a task.
- **Task Success Rate:** The percentage of tasks completed successfully.
- **Task Latency:** The time taken to process a task.
- **Resource Utilization:** The utilization of computational resources (CPU, memory, GPU).

Key Metrics for Monitoring Agent Performance:

- **Agent Accuracy:** The accuracy of an agent's decisions or predictions.
- **Agent Response Time:** The time taken by an agent to respond to a request.
- **Agent Resource Consumption:** The amount of computational resources consumed by an agent.

Monitoring Techniques:

- **Logging:** Log important events, errors, and performance metrics.
- **Visualization:** Visualize task progress, agent performance, and system metrics using dashboards and charts.
- **Real-time Monitoring:** Use real-time monitoring tools to track the system's performance.
- **Performance Profiling:** Identify performance bottlenecks and optimize the system accordingly.

Strategies for Improving Performance:

- **Dynamic Task Allocation:** Reassign tasks to agents based on their current workload and performance.
- **Load Balancing:** Distribute the workload evenly among agents to avoid overloading.
- **Adaptive Resource Allocation:** Adjust resource allocation to optimize performance.
- **Continuous Learning and Adaptation:** Enable agents to learn from their mistakes and improve their performance over time.

Understanding the Importance

Monitoring task progress and agent performance is crucial for ensuring the efficient and effective operation of a CrewAI system. It allows us to identify potential bottlenecks, optimize resource allocation, and improve overall system performance.

Key Metrics and Techniques:

Task Progress Monitoring

1. **Task Completion Time:** Track the time taken to complete each task.

- **Implementation:** Use timestamps to record the start and end times of each task.
- **Visualization:** Create a Gantt chart or timeline to visualize task progress.
2. **Task Success Rate:** Measure the percentage of tasks completed successfully.
    - **Implementation:** Log the success or failure of each task.
    - **Visualization:** Use a bar chart or pie chart to represent the success rate.
3. **Task Latency:** Measure the time taken to process a task.
    - **Implementation:** Log the time taken for each task phase (e.g., input, processing, output).
    - **Visualization:** Create a histogram or box plot to visualize the distribution of task latencies.

Agent Performance Monitoring

1. **Agent Accuracy:** Measure the accuracy of an agent's decisions or predictions.
    - **Implementation:** Compare the agent's output to the ground truth.
    - **Visualization:** Use a confusion matrix or ROC curve to visualize the agent's performance.
2. **Agent Response Time:** Measure the time taken by an agent to respond to a request.
    - **Implementation:** Log the time taken for each agent to process a task.
    - **Visualization:** Create a histogram or box plot to visualize the distribution of response times.
3. **Agent Resource Consumption:** Measure the amount of computational resources (CPU, memory, GPU) consumed by an agent.
    - **Implementation:** Use system monitoring tools to track resource usage.
    - **Visualization:** Create a line chart to visualize resource consumption over time.

Real-World Example: Monitoring a Self-Driving Car

- **Task Progress:** Monitor the progress of tasks like lane keeping, obstacle avoidance, and traffic light recognition.
- **Agent Performance:** Monitor the performance of perception agents (detecting objects), planning agents (generating driving plans), and control agents (executing actions).

Visualization Tools:

- **Dashboards:** Create custom dashboards to visualize key metrics and alerts.
- **Logging Tools:** Use tools like Logstash, Elasticsearch, and Kibana (ELK stack) to collect and analyze logs.
- **Monitoring Tools:** Use tools like Prometheus and Grafana to monitor system metrics and generate visualizations.

By effectively monitoring task progress and agent performance, we can identify bottlenecks, optimize resource allocation, and improve the overall performance of our CrewAI systems.

By effectively monitoring task progress and agent performance, we can identify areas for improvement and optimize the overall performance of the CrewAI system.

9.3 Dynamic Adjustment of Workflows

In a dynamic environment, CrewAI systems need to be able to adapt to changing conditions and adjust their workflows accordingly. Dynamic workflow adjustment allows the system to respond to unexpected events, optimize resource utilization, and improve overall performance.

Key Techniques for Dynamic Workflow Adjustment:

1. **Real-time Monitoring:**
    - Continuously monitor the system's performance and identify potential bottlenecks or issues.
    - Use metrics like task completion time, agent workload, and resource utilization.
2. **Adaptive Task Allocation:**

- Dynamically reassign tasks to agents based on their current workload and capabilities.
- Consider factors like agent availability, task priority, and resource constraints.

3. **Workflow Re-engineering:**
   - Modify the workflow to adapt to changes in the environment or requirements.
   - This may involve adding or removing tasks, changing the sequence of tasks, or adjusting the assignment of tasks to agents.

4. **Learning and Adaptation:**
   - Use machine learning techniques to learn from past performance and adapt the workflow.
   - For example, a system can learn to optimize task scheduling based on historical data.

Example: Dynamic Workflow Adjustment in a Self-Driving Car

- **Scenario:** A self-driving car encounters a traffic jam.
- **Dynamic Workflow Adjustment:**
  - The planning agent may re-route the vehicle to avoid the traffic jam.
  - The control agent may adjust the vehicle's speed and acceleration to optimize fuel consumption.
  - The perception agent may focus on monitoring the surrounding environment for potential hazards.

Challenges and Considerations:

- **Complexity:** Dynamic workflow adjustment can introduce complexity to the system.
- **Overhead:** Frequent adjustments may impact system performance.
- **Stability:** Changes to the workflow must be carefully considered to avoid unintended consequences.

By effectively implementing dynamic workflow adjustment, we can create more robust and adaptable CrewAI systems.

9.4 Tools for Tracking and Optimization

To effectively monitor and optimize CrewAI systems, various tools and techniques can be employed. Here are some of the most commonly used tools:

Monitoring Tools:

- **Prometheus:** An open-source monitoring system that collects metrics from various sources, including applications, systems, and infrastructure.
- **Grafana:** A powerful visualization tool that can be used to create dashboards to monitor the performance of CrewAI systems.
- **ELK Stack (Elasticsearch, Logstash, Kibana):** A popular tool stack for collecting, analyzing, and visualizing logs. It can be used to monitor system performance, identify errors, and track agent behavior.

Logging Tools:

- **Log4j:** A flexible logging framework for Java applications.
- **Python's logging module:** A built-in logging module for Python applications.
- **Structured Logging:** Log structured data (e.g., JSON) to facilitate analysis and visualization.

Performance Profiling Tools:

- **Profilers:** Tools like Python's cProfile or PyTorch Profiler can help identify performance bottlenecks in code.
- **Memory Profilers:** Tools like PyTorch's memory profiler can help identify memory leaks and optimize memory usage.

Machine Learning Experiment Tracking Tools:

- **MLflow:** A platform for managing the machine learning lifecycle, including experiment tracking, model registry, and deployment.

- **Weights & Biases:** A platform for tracking experiments, visualizing results, and collaborating with other researchers.

Optimization Techniques:

- **Hyperparameter Tuning:** Use techniques like grid search, random search, or Bayesian optimization to find optimal hyperparameters for models.
- **Model Pruning:** Remove unnecessary parameters from models to reduce computational cost and improve performance.
- **Quantization:** Reduce the precision of model weights to reduce memory footprint and accelerate inference.
- **Knowledge Distillation:** Transfer knowledge from a large, complex model to a smaller, faster model.

By effectively utilizing these tools and techniques, we can monitor the performance of CrewAI systems, identify areas for improvement, and optimize their behavior to achieve the desired outcomes.

Chapter 10 Conflict Resolution in Collaborative AI

10.1 Identifying Potential Conflicts Between Agents

In a collaborative AI system, conflicts between agents can arise due to various reasons, such as competing goals, resource constraints, or misunderstandings. Identifying these potential conflicts is crucial for effective conflict resolution.

Common Types of Conflicts

1. **Resource Conflicts:** Agents may compete for shared resources like CPU, memory, or network bandwidth.
2. **Goal Conflicts:** Agents may have conflicting goals or priorities.
3. **Communication Conflicts:** Misunderstandings or communication breakdowns can lead to conflicts.
4. **Dependency Conflicts:** Agents may rely on each other, and delays or failures in one agent can impact the others.

Techniques for Identifying Potential Conflicts:

1. **Static Analysis:**
   - Analyze the system's design and identify potential conflicts based on the agents' roles and responsibilities.
   - Consider the dependencies between agents and the potential for resource contention.
2. **Dynamic Analysis:**
   - Monitor the system's behavior during runtime to detect conflicts as they arise.
   - Use techniques like logging, profiling, and visualization to identify bottlenecks and inefficiencies.
3. **Conflict Simulation:**

- Simulate different scenarios to predict potential conflicts.
- Use simulation tools to test the system's robustness and identify weaknesses.

Example: Conflict in a Self-Driving Car

A self-driving car may encounter a situation where the perception agent detects a pedestrian crossing the road, while the planning agent has already planned a trajectory that would lead to a collision. This conflict can be identified through dynamic analysis and resolved by replanning the trajectory to avoid the pedestrian.

By proactively identifying potential conflicts, we can implement effective strategies to prevent or mitigate their impact on the system's performance.

10.2 Techniques for Resolving Agent Disputes

When conflicts arise between AI agents, effective techniques are needed to resolve these disputes and maintain the overall system's performance. Here are some common techniques:

1. Negotiation:

- Agents can negotiate with each other to find a mutually beneficial solution.
- This can involve bargaining, compromise, or arbitration.
- **Example:** Two agents competing for a shared resource can negotiate to share the resource or alternate its usage.

2. Mediation:

- A third-party agent can mediate the dispute.
- The mediator can analyze the situation, propose solutions, and facilitate negotiations.
- **Example:** A central control agent can intervene to resolve conflicts between lower-level agents.

3. Arbitration:

- A higher-authority agent can make a decision to resolve the conflict.
- This approach is suitable for critical situations where quick and decisive action is required.
- **Example:** A human operator can intervene to resolve a conflict that the AI agents cannot resolve themselves.

4. Prioritization:

- Prioritize tasks based on their importance and urgency.
- Agents can agree to defer lower-priority tasks to resolve more critical ones.
- **Example:** In a self-driving car, avoiding a collision is a higher priority than maintaining a specific speed.

5. Time-Sharing:

- Agents can share resources or alternate tasks over time.
- This approach can be used to balance the workload and prevent resource contention.
- **Example:** Two agents can share a computational resource by taking turns to use it.

6. Randomization:

- Randomly assign tasks or allocate resources to avoid systematic bias.
- This can help to prevent conflicts arising from deterministic decision-making.
- **Example:** Agents can randomly choose which task to perform next, reducing the likelihood of conflicts.

By understanding these techniques and applying them appropriately, we can minimize the impact of conflicts on the performance of CrewAI systems.

10.3 Managing Overlapping Tasks and Priorities

In complex CrewAI systems, agents may encounter situations where multiple tasks have overlapping deadlines or priorities.

Effective management of these overlapping tasks is crucial to ensure optimal system performance.

Key Strategies for Managing Overlapping Tasks and Priorities:

1. **Task Prioritization:**
    - **Prioritize tasks:** Assign priorities to tasks based on their importance and urgency.
    - **Dynamic Prioritization:** Re-evaluate priorities as the system's state changes.
    - **Consider resource constraints:** Account for limited resources when prioritizing tasks.
2. **Task Decomposition:**
    - Break down complex tasks into smaller, more manageable subtasks.
    - Assign subtasks to different agents to improve efficiency.
3. **Time Management:**
    - Use time management techniques like time-boxing and time estimation to allocate time to different tasks.
    - Monitor progress and adjust timelines as needed.
4. **Resource Allocation:**
    - Allocate resources (e.g., CPU, memory, network bandwidth) to tasks based on their priority and resource requirements.
    - Use dynamic resource allocation to adapt to changing conditions.
5. **Conflict Resolution:**
    - Develop strategies to resolve conflicts between tasks that compete for resources or attention.
    - Use techniques like negotiation, mediation, or arbitration.

Example: A Collaborative AI System for Autonomous Vehicles

In a self-driving car, multiple tasks may need to be performed simultaneously, such as:

- **Perception:** Detecting objects in the environment.
- **Planning:** Generating a safe and efficient driving plan.
- **Control:** Executing the driving plan.

To manage these overlapping tasks, the system can employ the following strategies:

- **Prioritize safety-critical tasks:** Tasks related to safety, such as obstacle avoidance, should be given higher priority.
- **Time-sharing:** Allocate resources to different tasks based on their urgency and importance.
- **Dynamic task scheduling:** Adjust the task schedule in real-time to respond to changing conditions.

By effectively managing overlapping tasks and priorities, we can ensure that CrewAI systems can operate efficiently and reliably in complex environments.

10.4 Case Study: Conflict Resolution in Practice

Scenario: A Collaborative AI System for Smart Grid Management

In a smart grid, multiple AI agents may be tasked with optimizing energy distribution, predicting demand, and managing renewable energy sources. Conflicts can arise when agents have conflicting objectives, such as maximizing energy efficiency versus minimizing costs.

Potential Conflicts:

- **Resource Contention:** Agents may compete for shared resources like communication bandwidth or computational power.
- **Conflicting Goals:** Agents may have conflicting goals, such as maximizing renewable energy usage versus minimizing carbon emissions.
- **Data Quality Issues:** Agents may rely on different data sources, leading to inconsistencies and conflicts.

Conflict Resolution Strategies:

1. **Centralized Control:** A central control agent can mediate conflicts and make decisions based on overall system goals.
2. **Distributed Negotiation:** Agents can negotiate with each other to find mutually beneficial solutions.
3. **Prioritization:** Agents can prioritize tasks based on their importance and urgency.
4. **Time-Sharing:** Agents can share resources and alternate tasks to avoid conflicts.
5. **Machine Learning:** Machine learning algorithms can be used to learn from past conflicts and optimize future decisions.

Example:

- **Conflict:** An energy storage agent wants to charge batteries during off-peak hours, while a demand response agent wants to discharge batteries to meet peak demand.
- **Resolution:** A higher-level agent can analyze the current energy grid conditions and make a decision based on factors like energy prices, renewable energy availability, and battery capacity.

Key Lessons:

- **Clear Communication:** Effective communication is essential for conflict resolution.
- **Shared Goals:** A shared understanding of the system's objectives can help to align agent behavior.
- **Flexibility and Adaptability:** The system should be able to adapt to changing conditions and resolve conflicts dynamically.
- **Human Oversight:** Human oversight can be valuable for resolving complex conflicts and making critical decisions.

By proactively identifying and addressing potential conflicts, we can ensure the smooth and efficient operation of CrewAI systems.

Chapter 11 Training and Improving AI Agents

11.1 Reinforcement Learning Techniques for Agent Training

Reinforcement learning (RL) is a powerful technique for training AI agents to make decisions in complex environments. In the context of CrewAI, RL can be used to train agents to collaborate effectively and achieve shared goals.

Key Concepts in Reinforcement Learning:

- **Agent:** An entity that interacts with an environment.
- **Environment:** The world in which the agent operates.
- **State:** The current situation or configuration of the environment.
- **Action:** A choice made by the agent to influence the environment.
- **Reward:** A numerical value assigned to a state-action pair, indicating the desirability of that action.

Reinforcement Learning Algorithms:

- **Q-Learning:** A model-free RL algorithm that learns the optimal action-value function, which estimates the expected reward for taking a specific action in a given state.
- **Deep Q-Networks (DQN):** A deep learning approach to Q-learning that uses neural networks to approximate the Q-value function.
- **Policy Gradient Methods:** These methods directly optimize the policy function, which maps states to actions.
- **Actor-Critic Methods:** Combine policy gradient methods with value function methods to improve learning efficiency.

Training CrewAI Agents with Reinforcement Learning:

1. **Define the Environment:**

- Create a simulated environment that mimics the real-world scenario.
- Define the state space, action space, and reward function.

2. **Initialize the Agent:**
   - Initialize the agent's parameters, such as weights and biases.
3. **Train the Agent:**
   - The agent interacts with the environment, taking actions and receiving rewards.
   - The agent uses the rewards to update its policy or value function.
4. **Evaluate the Agent:**
   - Periodically evaluate the agent's performance on a validation set.
   - Adjust the training process based on the evaluation results.

Example: Training a Collaborative Robot

A collaborative robot can be trained to work with a human worker to assemble products. The robot can learn to predict the human's actions, anticipate their needs, and coordinate its movements to avoid collisions.

Challenges and Considerations:

- **Exploration vs. Exploitation:** Balancing exploration (trying new actions) and exploitation (using known good actions).
- **Sparse Rewards:** Dealing with environments where rewards are infrequent or delayed.
- **Credit Assignment:** Assigning credit or blame to specific actions in a sequence of actions.
- **Generalization:** Enabling agents to generalize their knowledge to new situations.

By effectively applying reinforcement learning techniques, we can train intelligent agents that can collaborate effectively and achieve complex goals.

11.2 Transfer Learning and Fine-Tuning Pre-trained Models

Transfer learning is a powerful technique that leverages knowledge gained from one task to improve performance on a related task. In the context of CrewAI, transfer learning can be used to accelerate the training of agents and improve their performance.

Key Concepts in Transfer Learning:

- **Pre-trained Model:** A model that has been trained on a large dataset, often a general-purpose dataset like ImageNet.
- **Feature Extraction:** The process of extracting meaningful features from input data using a pre-trained model.
- **Fine-Tuning:** The process of adjusting the weights of a pre-trained model on a specific task.

Steps in Transfer Learning:

1. **Choose a Pre-trained Model:** Select a pre-trained model that is suitable for the target task.
2. **Freeze the Base Layers:** Freeze the weights of the earlier layers of the model to prevent them from being updated during training.
3. **Fine-Tune the Top Layers:** Train the top layers of the model on the target dataset.
4. **Unfreeze and Fine-Tune (Optional):** If necessary, unfreeze some of the earlier layers and fine-tune them along with the top layers.

Example: Transfer Learning for Image Classification

1. **Pre-train a Model on ImageNet:** Train a convolutional neural network (CNN) on a large dataset like ImageNet to classify images into thousands of categories.
2. **Freeze the Base Layers:** Freeze the convolutional layers of the pre-trained model.

3. **Add a New Classifier:** Add a new fully connected layer on top of the frozen layers to classify images into the desired categories.
4. **Fine-Tune the Model:** Train the new classifier layer using a smaller dataset of images from the target categories.

Understanding the Concept

Transfer learning is a technique where a model trained on one task is re-used as a starting point for a related task. This can significantly reduce training time and improve performance, especially when data is limited.

Step-by-Step Example: Image Classification

Task: Classify images of cats and dogs.

1. Choose a Pre-trained Model:

- Use a pre-trained model like ResNet50, which is trained on the ImageNet dataset.

2. Freeze the Base Layers:

- Freeze the convolutional layers of the ResNet50 model, as they have learned generic image features.

Python

```
import torch
import torchvision.models as models


model = models.resnet50(pretrained=True)


# Freeze the base layers
for param in model.parameters():
```

```
            param.requires_grad = False
```

3. **Add a New Classifier:**

    - Add a new fully connected layer on top of the frozen convolutional layers to classify images into two classes: cat or dog.

Python

```
num_ftrs = model.fc.in_features

model.fc = nn.Linear(num_ftrs, 2)
```

4. **Fine-Tune the Model:**

    - Create a dataset of cat and dog images.
    - Define a loss function (e.g., cross-entropy loss) and an optimizer (e.g., Adam).
    - Train the model on the new dataset, updating only the weights of the newly added classifier layer.

Python

```
   import torch.nn as nn

import torch.optim as optim


criterion = nn.CrossEntropyLoss()

optimizer = optim.Adam(model.parameters(), lr=0.001)


# ... training loop ...
```

Real-World Applications

- **Medical Image Analysis:** Pre-trained models can be used to classify medical images (e.g., X-rays, MRIs) into different categories, such as healthy or diseased.
- **Natural Language Processing:** Pre-trained language models like BERT and GPT-3 can be fine-tuned for tasks like text classification, sentiment analysis, and text generation.
- **Autonomous Driving:** Pre-trained models can be used to detect objects, track their movement, and predict their future trajectories.

Key Considerations

- **Data Quality:** The quality of the target dataset is crucial for successful transfer learning.
- **Hyperparameter Tuning:** Experiment with different hyperparameters (e.g., learning rate, batch size) to optimize performance.
- **Model Architecture:** Choose a pre-trained model that is suitable for the target task.
- **Domain Similarity:** The source and target domains should be similar to maximize the benefits of transfer learning.

By effectively utilizing transfer learning and fine-tuning, we can build powerful AI models with minimal training data and computational resources.

Benefits of Transfer Learning:

- **Faster Training:** Pre-trained models can significantly reduce training time.
- **Improved Performance:** Transfer learning can lead to better performance, especially when the target dataset is small or noisy.
- **Reduced Data Requirements:** Pre-trained models can be used with smaller datasets.

By effectively utilizing transfer learning, we can build more powerful and efficient CrewAI systems.

11.3 Continuous Learning and Adaptation in Dynamic Environments

In real-world scenarios, AI agents often operate in dynamic environments where conditions can change rapidly. To maintain their effectiveness, these agents must be capable of continuous learning and adaptation.

Key Techniques for Continuous Learning and Adaptation:

1. **Online Learning:**
   - Agents can learn from new data as it becomes available, without the need for retraining on the entire dataset.
   - This is particularly useful in non-stationary environments where data distributions change over time.
2. **Incremental Learning:**
   - Agents can learn new information incrementally, without forgetting previously learned knowledge.
   - This is important for systems that need to adapt to new tasks or concepts.
3. **Meta-Learning:**
   - Agents can learn to learn, enabling them to quickly adapt to new tasks or environments.
   - Meta-learning can be used to learn optimal learning strategies.
4. **Active Learning:**
   - Agents can actively select the most informative data to learn from, reducing the amount of data required for training.
   - This can be particularly useful in scenarios where data is limited or expensive to obtain.

Example: A Self-Driving Car

A self-driving car must be able to adapt to changing traffic conditions, weather conditions, and road infrastructure. To achieve this, the car's AI agents can use the following techniques:

- **Online Learning:** The car can learn from its experiences on the road, updating its models as it encounters new situations.
- **Incremental Learning:** The car can learn new driving strategies and techniques without forgetting previously learned knowledge.
- **Meta-Learning:** The car can learn to learn new driving skills, such as navigating through a construction zone or driving in heavy traffic.
- **Active Learning:** The car can actively seek out challenging driving scenarios to improve its performance.

Challenges and Considerations:

- **Catastrophic Forgetting:** Agents may forget previously learned knowledge when learning new information.
- **Concept Drift:** Data distributions may change over time, leading to performance degradation.
- **Computational Cost:** Continuous learning can be computationally expensive.

By effectively implementing these techniques, we can create AI agents that are capable of adapting to changing environments and continuously improving their performance.

Part IV
Practical Applications of CrewAI

Chapter 12 CrewAI in Business and Industry

12.1 How CrewAI is Transforming Different Sectors

CrewAI is revolutionizing various industries by enabling intelligent collaboration between multiple AI agents. Here are some key sectors where CrewAI is making a significant impact:

Healthcare

- **Medical Diagnosis:** AI agents can analyze medical images, patient records, and genetic data to identify diseases more accurately and efficiently.
- **Drug Discovery:** AI agents can collaborate to accelerate drug discovery processes by simulating molecular interactions and predicting drug efficacy.
- **Personalized Medicine:** AI agents can analyze patient data to develop personalized treatment plans.

Finance

- **Fraud Detection:** AI agents can work together to identify fraudulent transactions by analyzing various data sources.
- **Algorithmic Trading:** AI agents can collaborate to make complex trading decisions in real-time.
- **Risk Assessment:** AI agents can assess financial risks by analyzing market trends and economic indicators.

Manufacturing

- **Predictive Maintenance:** AI agents can predict equipment failures and optimize maintenance schedules.
- **Quality Control:** AI agents can inspect products for defects and ensure quality standards.

- **Supply Chain Optimization:** AI agents can optimize supply chain operations, reducing costs and improving efficiency.

Retail

- **Customer Service:** AI agents can provide personalized customer service through chatbots and virtual assistants.
- **Demand Forecasting:** AI agents can analyze sales data to predict future demand and optimize inventory management.
- **Recommendation Systems:** AI agents can recommend products to customers based on their preferences and purchase history.

Transportation and Logistics

- **Autonomous Vehicles:** AI agents can collaborate to control self-driving cars and trucks.
- **Logistics Optimization:** AI agents can optimize transportation routes and schedules to reduce costs and improve efficiency.
- **Traffic Management:** AI agents can analyze traffic data to optimize traffic flow and reduce congestion.

By harnessing the power of collaboration, CrewAI is driving innovation and improving the efficiency and effectiveness of various industries.

12.2 Applications in Ecommerce, Customer Support, and Operations

CrewAI is transforming the way businesses operate in various sectors, including e-commerce, customer support, and operations.

E-commerce

- **Personalized Product Recommendations:** AI agents can analyze customer behavior and preferences to recommend personalized products.

- **Dynamic Pricing:** AI agents can optimize pricing strategies based on real-time market conditions and customer demand.
- **Inventory Management:** AI agents can predict demand and optimize inventory levels to reduce stockouts and overstock.
- **Fraud Detection:** AI agents can detect fraudulent transactions and protect businesses from losses.

Customer Support

- **Chatbots and Virtual Assistants:** AI agents can provide 24/7 customer support, answering questions, resolving issues, and providing product information.
- **Sentiment Analysis:** AI agents can analyze customer feedback to identify areas for improvement.
- **Customer Segmentation:** AI agents can segment customers based on their behavior and preferences to tailor marketing campaigns.

Operations

- **Supply Chain Optimization:** AI agents can optimize supply chain operations, reducing costs and improving efficiency.
- **Predictive Maintenance:** AI agents can predict equipment failures and schedule maintenance to minimize downtime.
- **Quality Control:** AI agents can automate quality control processes, ensuring product quality and consistency.
- **Process Automation:** AI agents can automate routine tasks, freeing up human workers to focus on more strategic activities.

By leveraging CrewAI, businesses can improve customer satisfaction, reduce costs, and gain a competitive edge.

12.3 Case Studies of Successful CrewAI Implementations

While CrewAI is a relatively new field, there are several notable examples of successful implementations that showcase its potential.

1. Autonomous Vehicles

- **Collaboration of AI Agents:** Multiple AI agents work together to perceive the environment, plan the vehicle's path, and control its movement.
- **Benefits:** Improved safety, reduced traffic congestion, and increased accessibility.

2. Healthcare

- **Medical Image Analysis:** AI agents can analyze medical images (X-rays, CT scans, MRIs) to detect diseases like cancer and heart disease.
- **Drug Discovery:** AI agents can accelerate drug discovery by simulating molecular interactions and predicting drug efficacy.
- **Personalized Medicine:** AI agents can analyze patient data to develop personalized treatment plans.

3. Customer Service

- **Virtual Assistants:** AI-powered virtual assistants can handle customer inquiries, provide product information, and resolve issues.
- **Sentiment Analysis:** AI agents can analyze customer feedback to identify areas for improvement.
- **Chatbots:** AI-powered chatbots can engage with customers, answer questions, and provide support.

4. Financial Services

- **Fraud Detection:** AI agents can analyze financial transactions to identify fraudulent activity.

- **Algorithmic Trading:** AI agents can make automated trading decisions based on market data and predictive models.
- **Risk Assessment:** AI agents can assess credit risk and investment risk.

5. Supply Chain Management

- **Demand Forecasting:** AI agents can predict future demand to optimize inventory levels.
- **Logistics Optimization:** AI agents can optimize transportation routes and schedules to reduce costs and improve efficiency.
- **Quality Control:** AI agents can inspect products for defects and ensure quality standards.

By learning from these successful case studies, we can gain valuable insights into the potential of CrewAI and its applications in various industries. As technology continues to advance, we can expect to see even more innovative and impactful CrewAI systems in the future.

Chapter 13 Advanced Use Cases in Research and Development

13.1 Using CrewAI for Scientific Research and Data Analysis

CrewAI can revolutionize scientific research and data analysis by enabling collaborative problem-solving and accelerating discovery. Here are some key applications:

1. Accelerating Scientific Discovery:

- **Drug Discovery:** AI agents can analyze vast amounts of biological data to identify potential drug targets and design novel drug molecules.
- **Material Science:** AI agents can predict the properties of materials and design new materials with desired properties.
- **Climate Modeling:** AI agents can analyze climate data to improve climate models and predict future climate trends.

2. Enhancing Data Analysis:

- **Feature Engineering:** AI agents can automatically discover and engineer relevant features from raw data.
- **Data Cleaning and Preprocessing:** AI agents can identify and correct errors in data, improving data quality.
- **Data Visualization:** AI agents can create informative visualizations to help researchers understand complex data.

3. Collaborative Research:

- **Remote Collaboration:** AI agents can facilitate collaboration between researchers located in different parts of the world.
- **Knowledge Sharing:** AI agents can share knowledge and insights, accelerating the pace of discovery.
- **Experiment Design:** AI agents can help researchers design experiments and optimize experimental parameters.

Example: A Collaborative AI System for Cancer Research

- **Image Analysis Agent:** Analyzes medical images to identify tumor cells.
- **Natural Language Processing Agent:** Extracts information from medical literature to identify potential treatment strategies.
- **Machine Learning Agent:** Develops predictive models to predict patient outcomes.
- **Knowledge Base Agent:** Stores and retrieves relevant medical knowledge.

These agents can collaborate to accelerate drug discovery, improve patient diagnosis, and develop personalized treatment plans.

13.2 Collaborative AI for Innovation and Prototyping

Collaborative AI can significantly accelerate innovation and prototyping by enabling rapid experimentation, idea generation, and design optimization. Here are some key applications:

1. Design and Engineering:

- **Generative Design:** AI agents can generate innovative designs by exploring a vast design space.
- **Simulation and Optimization:** AI agents can simulate and optimize designs to improve performance and reduce costs.
- **Collaborative Design:** AI agents can collaborate with human designers to create innovative products.

2. Software Development:

- **Automated Code Generation:** AI agents can generate code snippets or entire functions based on natural language specifications.
- **Code Optimization:** AI agents can identify and optimize performance bottlenecks in code.
- **Test Automation:** AI agents can automate testing processes to improve software quality.

3. **Product Development:**

- **Rapid Prototyping:** AI agents can accelerate the prototyping process by automating design and manufacturing tasks.
- **Product Testing:** AI agents can simulate product performance in different environments and identify potential issues.
- **Product Customization:** AI agents can customize products to meet individual customer needs.

Example: A Collaborative AI System for Product Design

- **Design Generation Agent:** Generates initial design concepts based on user requirements.
- **Simulation Agent:** Simulates the performance of the design under various conditions.
- **Optimization Agent:** Optimizes the design to improve performance and reduce costs.
- **Manufacturing Agent:** Generates manufacturing instructions for the optimized design.

By collaborating with human designers and engineers, these AI agents can accelerate the product development process and create innovative products.

CrewAI has the potential to revolutionize innovation and prototyping by enabling rapid experimentation, optimization, and the creation of novel solutions.

13.3 Real-World Examples from Leading Research Labs

Several leading research labs are actively exploring the potential of CrewAI to advance scientific research and technological innovation. Here are some notable examples:

OpenAI

- **Reinforcement Learning:** OpenAI has developed sophisticated reinforcement learning algorithms that enable AI agents to learn complex tasks through trial and error.
- **Language Models:** OpenAI's language models, such as GPT-3, can generate human-quality text, translate languages, and write different kinds of creative content.

Google AI

- **Medical AI:** Google AI is developing AI systems to assist in medical diagnosis, drug discovery, and personalized medicine.
- **Quantum AI:** Google AI is exploring the potential of quantum computing to solve complex problems that are intractable for classical computers.

Microsoft Research

- **AI for Accessibility:** Microsoft Research is developing AI systems to help people with disabilities, such as speech recognition and text-to-speech technologies.
- **Responsible AI:** Microsoft Research is working on developing AI systems that are fair, transparent, and accountable.

Stanford AI Lab

- **Human-Centered AI:** Stanford AI Lab focuses on developing AI systems that are beneficial to humanity.
- **AI for Social Good:** Researchers at Stanford are working on AI applications for social good, such as education, healthcare, and environmental conservation.

UC Berkeley AI Research

- **Autonomous Systems:** UC Berkeley is developing autonomous robots and vehicles.
- **Human-AI Interaction:** Researchers at UC Berkeley are exploring ways to improve human-AI interaction.

These are just a few examples of the many ways in which leading research labs are leveraging CrewAI to push the boundaries of technology and address global challenges. As AI technology continues to advance, we can expect to see even more innovative and impactful applications of CrewAI in the future.

Chapter 14 Developing Custom CrewAI Solutions

14.1 When to Build Custom Solutions vs. Using Out-of-the-Box Tools

The decision to build a custom CrewAI solution or use an out-of-the-box tool depends on various factors, including the specific requirements of the project, the available resources, and the desired level of customization.

Build a Custom Solution When:

- **Unique Requirements:** If your project has unique requirements that cannot be met by existing tools, building a custom solution is necessary.
- **High Level of Customization:** You need a highly customized solution to fit your specific needs.
- **Deep Integration:** The solution needs to be tightly integrated with your existing systems and workflows.
- **Long-Term Vision:** You have a long-term vision for the project and want to build a solution that can evolve over time.

Use an Out-of-the-Box Tool When:

- **Time Constraints:** You need a quick solution and don't have the time or resources to build a custom solution from scratch.
- **Limited Resources:** You have limited budget or technical expertise.
- **Standard Use Cases:** Your project fits a common use case that can be addressed with existing tools.
- **Rapid Prototyping:** You want to quickly prototype and test ideas.

Key Considerations:

- **Cost:** Building a custom solution can be more expensive than using an out-of-the-box tool, especially in terms of development and maintenance costs.
- **Time:** Building a custom solution may take longer than using an out-of-the-box tool.
- **Expertise:** Building a custom solution requires specialized skills and knowledge.
- **Flexibility:** Custom solutions offer greater flexibility but may require more ongoing maintenance.
- **Scalability:** Both custom solutions and out-of-the-box tools can be scaled, but the approach may differ.

By carefully considering these factors, you can make an informed decision about whether to build a custom CrewAI solution or use an out-of-the-box tool.

14.2 Introduction to Customizing Agents for Specific Tasks

Customizing AI agents for specific tasks involves tailoring their architecture, training data, and algorithms to achieve optimal performance. This allows for the creation of highly specialized agents that can excel in their respective domains.

Key Aspects of Agent Customization

1. **Architecture Selection:**
    - **Neural Network Architectures:** Choose appropriate architectures like CNNs, RNNs, or Transformers based on the task.
    - **Hybrid Architectures:** Combine multiple architectures to create more powerful agents.
2. **Data Preparation and Augmentation:**
    - Collect and clean relevant data.
    - Augment data to increase diversity and improve model generalization.
3. **Model Training:**
    - Train models using suitable algorithms and optimization techniques.

- Fine-tune pre-trained models to adapt them to specific tasks.
4. **Hyperparameter Tuning:**
    - Experiment with different hyperparameters to optimize model performance.
5. **Evaluation and Validation:**
    - Evaluate model performance using appropriate metrics and validation sets.
    - Iterate on the training process to improve performance.

Common Customization Techniques

- **Transfer Learning:** Use pre-trained models as a starting point and fine-tune them on specific tasks.
- **Meta-Learning:** Train agents to learn how to learn, allowing them to adapt to new tasks quickly.
- **Reinforcement Learning:** Train agents to make decisions through trial and error, maximizing rewards.
- **Multi-Task Learning:** Train agents on multiple related tasks simultaneously, improving generalization and performance.

By carefully customizing AI agents, we can create powerful and versatile systems capable of tackling a wide range of complex tasks.

14.3 Integrating CrewAI with Other Business Systems

Integrating CrewAI systems with existing business systems is essential to leverage their full potential. This integration allows for seamless data exchange, automation of workflows, and enhanced decision-making.

Key Integration Strategies:

1. **API Integration:**
    - Use APIs to connect CrewAI systems with other software applications.

- This allows for data exchange and automated workflows.
2. **Data Integration:**
   - Establish data pipelines to move data between CrewAI systems and other systems.
   - Ensure data consistency and quality.
3. **User Interface Integration:**
   - Integrate CrewAI systems with existing user interfaces to provide a seamless user experience.
4. **Security and Privacy:**
   - Implement robust security measures to protect sensitive data.
   - Adhere to data privacy regulations.

Challenges and Considerations:

- **Data Compatibility:** Ensure data formats and structures are compatible.
- **Security Risks:** Address potential security vulnerabilities.
- **Performance Impact:** Minimize the impact of integration on system performance.
- **Complexity:** Integration can be complex, especially for large-scale systems.

Example: Integrating a CrewAI System with a CRM System

1. **Data Integration:**
   - Extract customer data from the CRM system and feed it into the CrewAI system for analysis.
   - Use APIs to send customer information to the CRM system.
2. **Workflow Integration:**
   - Automate customer support tasks, such as ticket creation and resolution.
   - Use AI-powered chatbots to handle customer inquiries.
3. **User Interface Integration:**
   - Integrate the CrewAI system with the CRM system's user interface to provide a seamless experience for customer service agents.

By effectively integrating CrewAI systems with other business systems, organizations can unlock new opportunities, improve efficiency, and drive innovation.

14.4 Example of a Customized CrewAI Solution

Scenario: A Personalized E-commerce Platform

Let's consider an e-commerce platform that aims to provide highly personalized shopping experiences. To achieve this, a custom CrewAI solution can be implemented.

Key Components of the CrewAI System:

1. **Customer Profile Agent:**
   - Collects and analyzes customer data, including purchase history, browsing behavior, and demographic information.
   - Creates detailed customer profiles to understand their preferences and needs.
2. **Product Recommendation Agent:**
   - Utilizes collaborative filtering and content-based filtering techniques to recommend products tailored to individual customers.
   - Leverages machine learning algorithms to learn from customer behavior and improve recommendations over time.
3. **Personalized Marketing Agent:**
   - Develops targeted marketing campaigns based on customer segments and preferences.
   - Uses A/B testing to optimize marketing strategies.
4. **Customer Support Agent:**
   - Provides personalized customer support through chatbots and virtual assistants.
   - Utilizes natural language processing to understand customer queries and provide relevant answers.

How the Agents Collaborate:

1. **Customer Profile Agent** shares customer data with the **Product Recommendation Agent** and **Personalized Marketing Agent**.
2. **Product Recommendation Agent** generates personalized product recommendations based on customer profiles and preferences.
3. **Personalized Marketing Agent** develops targeted marketing campaigns based on customer segments and preferences.
4. **Customer Support Agent** interacts with customers, answering queries and resolving issues.

Benefits of a Customized CrewAI Solution:

- **Enhanced Customer Experience:** Personalized product recommendations, tailored marketing campaigns, and efficient customer support can significantly improve customer satisfaction.
- **Increased Sales:** By understanding customer preferences and behavior, the platform can increase sales and revenue.
- **Reduced Costs:** Automation of tasks like customer support and inventory management can reduce operational costs.
- **Competitive Advantage:** A personalized and efficient e-commerce platform can give a competitive edge over traditional retailers.

By tailoring a CrewAI solution to specific business needs, e-commerce platforms can achieve significant improvements in customer engagement, sales, and overall business performance.

Part V

Best Practices and Future Directions

Chapter 15 Best Practices for CrewAI Success

15.1 Tips for Effective Collaboration and Efficiency

Effective collaboration is essential for the success of any CrewAI system. By following these tips, you can enhance collaboration and improve the efficiency of your AI agents:

1. Clear Communication Channels

- **Establish clear communication protocols:** Define the channels and methods for agents to communicate with each other.
- **Use standardized formats:** Use consistent data formats and communication protocols to facilitate interoperability.
- **Monitor communication channels:** Regularly monitor communication channels to identify and resolve issues.

2. Well-Defined Roles and Responsibilities

- **Assign clear roles:** Clearly define the roles and responsibilities of each agent.
- **Avoid overlapping responsibilities:** Ensure that there is no duplication of effort.
- **Establish a hierarchy:** Define a clear hierarchy of agents to facilitate decision-making and conflict resolution.

3. Effective Task Allocation

- **Prioritize tasks:** Assign higher priority to tasks that are critical to the overall goal.
- **Consider agent capabilities:** Assign tasks to agents that are best suited to perform them.
- **Dynamic task allocation:** Adjust task assignments as needed to adapt to changing conditions.

4. Continuous Monitoring and Optimization

- **Monitor agent performance:** Track metrics such as accuracy, speed, and resource utilization.
- **Identify bottlenecks:** Identify and address bottlenecks in the workflow.
- **Optimize resource allocation:** Allocate resources efficiently to maximize performance.

5. Collaboration and Teamwork

- **Encourage collaboration:** Foster a culture of collaboration and knowledge sharing among agents.
- **Promote teamwork:** Encourage agents to work together to achieve common goals.
- **Resolve conflicts:** Develop effective strategies for resolving conflicts between agents.

By following these tips, you can create CrewAI systems that are efficient, effective, and capable of achieving complex goals.

15.2 Managing Resource Use and Cost Efficiency

Efficient resource utilization is crucial for the successful deployment and operation of CrewAI systems. By managing resource usage effectively, we can reduce costs, improve performance, and ensure sustainability.

Key Strategies for Managing Resource Use and Cost Efficiency:

1. Resource Allocation:

- **Dynamic Resource Allocation:** Allocate resources to agents based on their current workload and the importance of their tasks.
- **Resource Sharing:** Share resources among agents to optimize utilization.
- **Resource Prioritization:** Prioritize resource allocation to critical tasks.

2. Energy Efficiency:

- **Energy-Efficient Hardware:** Use energy-efficient hardware components.
- **Power Management:** Implement power-saving techniques, such as sleep and hibernation modes.
- **Dynamic Voltage and Frequency Scaling (DVFS):** Adjust the CPU's voltage and frequency to optimize performance and power consumption.

3. Cloud-Based Solutions:

- **Leverage Cloud Computing:** Utilize cloud-based infrastructure to reduce upfront costs and scale resources as needed.
- **Serverless Computing:** Use serverless functions to automatically scale resources based on demand.

4. Optimization Techniques:

- **Model Compression:** Reduce the size of models by techniques like pruning, quantization, and knowledge distillation.
- **Efficient Algorithms:** Use efficient algorithms and data structures to minimize computational complexity.
- **Parallel and Distributed Computing:** Distribute computations across multiple devices or servers to accelerate processing.

5. Monitoring and Optimization:

- **Continuous Monitoring:** Monitor resource usage and identify bottlenecks.
- **Performance Profiling:** Analyze the performance of different components to identify optimization opportunities.
- **Automated Optimization:** Use machine learning techniques to automate the optimization process.

By implementing these strategies, we can build CrewAI systems that are both cost-effective and high-performing.

15.3 Improving Agent Communication and Coordination

Effective communication and coordination are essential for the success of any CrewAI system. By optimizing these aspects, we can enhance the overall performance and efficiency of the system.

Key Strategies for Improving Agent Communication and Coordination:

1. Clear Communication Protocols

- **Standardized Formats:** Use standardized data formats and protocols to ensure seamless communication.
- **Error Handling:** Implement robust error handling mechanisms to address communication failures.
- **Asynchronous Communication:** Employ asynchronous communication techniques to improve scalability and reduce latency.

2. Efficient Information Sharing

- **Shared Knowledge Bases:** Establish shared knowledge bases to facilitate information sharing.
- **Centralized Coordination:** Use a central controller to coordinate agent activities and resolve conflicts.
- **Decentralized Coordination:** Enable agents to make local decisions and coordinate with their peers.

3. Collaborative Learning

- **Knowledge Transfer:** Encourage knowledge sharing and learning between agents.
- **Joint Learning:** Train multiple agents on a shared task to improve their collective performance.
- **Multi-Agent Reinforcement Learning:** Use reinforcement learning to train agents to collaborate effectively.

4. Conflict Resolution Mechanisms

- **Negotiation:** Allow agents to negotiate and compromise to resolve conflicts.
- **Mediation:** Use a third-party agent to mediate disputes and facilitate agreement.
- **Arbitration:** A higher-level authority can make decisions to resolve conflicts.

5. Monitoring and Optimization

- **Monitor Communication Patterns:** Track communication patterns to identify bottlenecks and inefficiencies.
- **Optimize Communication Protocols:** Adjust communication protocols to improve performance and reduce overhead.
- **Adapt to Changing Conditions:** Continuously monitor the environment and adjust communication strategies accordingly.

By implementing these strategies, we can improve the communication and coordination between AI agents, leading to more efficient and effective CrewAI systems.

15.4 Security and Privacy Best Practices

As CrewAI systems become increasingly complex and interconnected, ensuring their security and privacy is paramount. Here are some best practices to protect your CrewAI systems:

1. Data Security:

- **Data Encryption:** Encrypt sensitive data both at rest and in transit.
- **Access Controls:** Implement strong access controls to limit access to authorized personnel.
- **Regular Security Audits:** Conduct regular security audits to identify vulnerabilities.
- **Data Privacy Compliance:** Adhere to relevant data privacy regulations (e.g., GDPR, CCPA).

2. Network Security:

- **Secure Network Protocols:** Use secure protocols like HTTPS and SSH.
- **Firewall Protection:** Implement firewalls to protect the system from unauthorized access.
- **Intrusion Detection and Prevention Systems (IDS/IPS):** Monitor network traffic for malicious activity.

3. Agent Security:

- **Input Validation:** Validate input data to prevent malicious attacks.
- **Output Sanitization:** Sanitize output to avoid unintended consequences.
- **Regular Updates and Patches:** Keep agents and their underlying software up-to-date.

4. Ethical Considerations:

- **Bias Mitigation:** Develop algorithms that are fair and unbiased.
- **Transparency:** Make AI systems transparent and explainable.
- **Accountability:** Establish accountability for the actions of AI systems.

5. Incident Response Plan:

- **Incident Response Team:** Form a dedicated team to respond to security incidents.
- **Incident Response Procedures:** Develop procedures for detecting, responding to, and recovering from security breaches.
- **Regular Testing:** Conduct regular security testing to identify vulnerabilities.

By following these best practices, you can build secure and trustworthy CrewAI systems that protect sensitive data and mitigate potential risks.

Chapter 16 Ethical and Social Considerations

16.1 Addressing Bias and Fairness in CrewAI Systems

AI systems, including CrewAI, can inadvertently perpetuate and amplify biases present in the data they are trained on. This can lead to unfair and discriminatory outcomes. It's crucial to address bias and fairness to ensure that AI systems are ethical and equitable.

Key Strategies to Address Bias and Fairness:

1. **Fair Data Collection and Curation:**
   - **Diverse and Representative Datasets:** Ensure that training data is diverse and representative of the population it will serve.
   - **Data Quality:** Clean and preprocess data to remove biases and errors.
2. **Algorithmic Fairness:**
   - **Fairness Metrics:** Use fairness metrics to evaluate the fairness of AI models.
   - **Fairness-Aware Algorithms:** Develop algorithms that explicitly consider fairness constraints.
3. **Bias Detection and Mitigation:**
   - **Identify Biases:** Use techniques like statistical analysis and visualization to identify biases in data and models.
   - **Mitigate Biases:** Implement strategies like re-weighting, re-sampling, and adversarial debiasing to reduce bias.
4. **Transparency and Explainability:**
   - **Model Interpretability:** Develop models that are interpretable and explainable.
   - **Transparency in Decision-Making:** Provide clear explanations for the decisions made by AI systems.

5. **Human Oversight:**
   - **Human Review:** Have human experts review and validate the outputs of AI systems.
   - **Ethical Guidelines:** Establish ethical guidelines for the development and deployment of AI systems.

Example: Facial Recognition Bias

Facial recognition systems have been shown to be biased against certain demographic groups, particularly people of color. To address this issue, researchers and developers can:

- **Collect Diverse Datasets:** Use datasets that include a diverse range of faces.
- **Develop Fair Algorithms:** Use algorithms that are less susceptible to bias.
- **Regularly Test and Monitor:** Continuously test and monitor the system for bias.

By addressing bias and fairness, we can ensure that CrewAI systems are used ethically and responsibly.

16.2 Privacy and Data Protection in Collaborative AI

As CrewAI systems increasingly rely on data, it is crucial to prioritize privacy and data protection. Here are some key considerations:

Data Privacy:

- **Data Minimization:** Collect and process only the necessary data.
- **Anonymization and Pseudonymization:** Remove or mask personally identifiable information.
- **Data Encryption:** Encrypt sensitive data to protect it from unauthorized access.

- **Secure Data Storage:** Store data securely and implement access controls.

Data Security:

- **Network Security:** Protect the network infrastructure with firewalls and intrusion detection systems.
- **Secure Communication:** Use secure communication protocols to protect data transmission.
- **Regular Security Audits:** Conduct regular security audits to identify and address vulnerabilities.
- **Incident Response Plan:** Have a plan in place to respond to security incidents.

Ethical Considerations:

- **Transparency:** Be transparent about data collection and usage practices.
- **Fairness:** Ensure that AI systems are fair and unbiased.
- **Accountability:** Establish accountability for the decisions made by AI systems.

Legal Compliance:

- **Data Protection Laws:** Adhere to relevant data protection laws, such as GDPR and CCPA.
- **Consent Management:** Obtain explicit consent from individuals before collecting and processing their data.

Best Practices:

- **Privacy by Design:** Incorporate privacy considerations into the design and development of AI systems.
- **Data Minimization:** Collect only the necessary data to achieve the desired outcome.
- **Secure Data Storage:** Store data securely and implement access controls.
- **Regular Security Audits:** Conduct regular security audits to identify and address vulnerabilities.

- **Transparent Data Practices:** Be transparent about data collection, usage, and sharing practices.
- **User Control:** Provide users with control over their data, including the ability to access, modify, and delete their data.

By following these guidelines, we can develop CrewAI systems that are both powerful and responsible.

16.3 Ensuring Transparency and Accountability

Transparency and accountability are crucial for building trust in AI systems. Here are some strategies to ensure transparency and accountability in CrewAI systems:

Transparency:

- **Explainable AI:** Develop models that can explain their decision-making processes.
- **Feature Importance Analysis:** Identify the most important features that influence the model's predictions.
- **Visualizations:** Use visualizations to explain complex models and their outputs.
- **Documentation:** Document the development process, data sources, and model assumptions.

Accountability:

- **Human Oversight:** Implement human oversight to monitor and control AI systems.
- **Ethical Guidelines:** Develop and adhere to ethical guidelines for AI development and deployment.
- **Bias Mitigation:** Actively identify and mitigate biases in data and algorithms.
- **Error Handling:** Implement robust error handling mechanisms to prevent unintended consequences.

Real-World Example: Autonomous Vehicles

- **Transparency:** Explain the decision-making process of the self-driving car, such as how it perceives the environment, makes decisions, and executes actions.

- **Accountability:** Assign responsibility for accidents and incidents involving autonomous vehicles.
- **Bias Mitigation:** Ensure that the AI systems are trained on diverse datasets to avoid biases against certain groups of people.

By prioritizing transparency and accountability, we can build AI systems that are trustworthy and beneficial to society.

16.4 Ethical Case Studies and Best Practices

As AI technology advances, it is essential to consider the ethical implications of its use. By understanding ethical case studies and best practices, we can develop responsible and beneficial CrewAI systems.

Ethical Case Studies

1. **Algorithmic Bias:**
    - **Problem:** AI algorithms can perpetuate biases present in the training data, leading to unfair outcomes.
    - **Solution:** Use diverse and representative datasets, employ fairness metrics, and regularly audit algorithms for bias.
2. **Job Displacement:**
    - **Problem:** AI automation can lead to job losses.
    - **Solution:** Invest in retraining and upskilling programs to help workers adapt to the changing job market.
3. **Privacy Concerns:**
    - **Problem:** AI systems can collect and process large amounts of personal data, raising privacy concerns.
    - **Solution:** Implement strong data privacy measures, including data minimization, anonymization, and encryption.
4. **Autonomous Weapons:**
    - **Problem:** Autonomous weapons systems raise ethical concerns about the potential for unintended harm.

- **Solution:** Develop international regulations and guidelines to govern the development and use of autonomous weapons.

Best Practices for Ethical AI

1. **Human-Centered AI:** Design AI systems that prioritize human values and well-being.
2. **Transparency and Explainability:** Make AI systems transparent and understandable to humans.
3. **Fairness and Non-Discrimination:** Ensure that AI systems are fair and unbiased.
4. **Privacy by Design:** Incorporate privacy considerations into the design and development of AI systems.
5. **Accountability:** Establish clear accountability for the decisions and actions of AI systems.
6. **Continuous Monitoring and Evaluation:** Monitor the performance and impact of AI systems and make necessary adjustments.
7. **Ethical Guidelines:** Develop and adhere to ethical guidelines for AI development and deployment.
8. **Collaboration and Stakeholder Engagement:** Collaborate with stakeholders to ensure that AI is developed and used responsibly.

By considering these ethical principles and best practices, we can build AI systems that benefit society and minimize potential harm.

Chapter 17 Monitoring and Debugging CrewAI Systems

17.1 Identifying and Troubleshooting Common Issues

Common Issues in CrewAI Systems:

- **Performance Bottlenecks:** Slow execution times, high resource utilization, or latency issues.
- **Communication Failures:** Errors in message passing or synchronization between agents.
- **Data Quality Issues:** Incorrect, missing, or inconsistent data.
- **Agent Failures:** Individual agents may malfunction or fail to perform their tasks.
- **System Instability:** Unpredictable behavior or crashes.

Troubleshooting Techniques:

1. **Logging:**
   - Log detailed information about the system's behavior, including agent actions, decisions, and errors.
   - Use a centralized logging system to collect and analyze logs from multiple agents.
2. **Monitoring:**
   - Monitor system performance metrics, such as CPU usage, memory usage, and network traffic.
   - Use visualization tools to identify trends and anomalies.
3. **Debugging:**
   - Use debugging tools to step through code and inspect variables.
   - Set breakpoints to pause execution and analyze the system's state.
4. **Profiling:**

- Identify performance bottlenecks using profiling tools.
- Optimize code and algorithms to improve performance.
5. **Testing:**
    - Conduct unit tests, integration tests, and end-to-end tests to identify and fix bugs.
    - Use simulation environments to test the system under different conditions.

Example: Troubleshooting a Communication Failure

If agents are experiencing communication failures, consider the following:

- **Check Network Connectivity:** Ensure that agents can communicate with each other and the central server.
- **Inspect Message Queues:** Verify that messages are being processed and delivered correctly.
- **Review Log Files:** Look for error messages or exceptions related to communication.
- **Test Communication Protocols:** Simulate different network conditions to identify potential issues.

By effectively identifying and troubleshooting issues, we can ensure the reliability and performance of CrewAI systems.

17.2 Monitoring Agent Performance and System Health

Monitoring the performance and health of AI agents is crucial for the overall success of a CrewAI system. By tracking key metrics and using effective monitoring tools, we can identify potential issues early on and take corrective actions.

Key Metrics to Monitor:

1. **Agent Performance:**
    - **Accuracy:** Measure the accuracy of agent decisions and predictions.

- **Precision and Recall:** Evaluate the precision and recall of agent outputs.
- **Response Time:** Monitor the time taken by agents to process tasks.
- **Resource Utilization:** Track the CPU, memory, and GPU usage of agents.
2. **System Health:**
    - **Network Latency:** Monitor network latency to ensure efficient communication between agents.
    - **Server Load:** Track server load to prevent overloading and system failures.
    - **Data Integrity:** Verify the integrity of data stored and processed by the system.

Monitoring Tools and Techniques:

1. **Logging:**
    - Log agent actions, decisions, and errors.
    - Analyze logs to identify patterns and anomalies.
2. **Visualization:**
    - Use visualization tools to monitor system performance and identify trends.
    - Create dashboards to display key metrics.
3. **Profiling:**
    - Profile agent code to identify performance bottlenecks.
    - Optimize code to improve efficiency.
4. **Alerting:**
    - Set up alerts to notify administrators of critical issues.
    - Use automated alerting systems to proactively address problems.

Best Practices for Monitoring:

- **Continuous Monitoring:** Monitor the system continuously to detect issues early.
- **Real-time Monitoring:** Use real-time monitoring tools to track system performance.
- **Historical Data Analysis:** Analyze historical data to identify trends and patterns.

- **Automated Anomaly Detection:** Use machine learning techniques to automatically detect anomalies.
- **Regular Review and Optimization:** Regularly review monitoring data and make necessary adjustments to improve system performance.

By effectively monitoring agent performance and system health, we can ensure the reliability, efficiency, and effectiveness of CrewAI systems.

17.3 Debugging Techniques for Collaborative AI Systems

Debugging collaborative AI systems can be challenging due to their complexity and the interdependence of multiple agents. However, with the right techniques and tools, we can effectively identify and resolve issues.

Key Debugging Techniques:

1. **Logging:**
    - **Detailed Logging:** Log detailed information about each agent's actions, decisions, and internal states.
    - **Time-Stamped Logs:** Include timestamps to correlate events across different agents.
    - **Error Logging:** Log errors, exceptions, and warnings to identify potential issues.
2. **Visualization:**
    - **Visualize Data:** Use visualization tools to visualize data flows, agent interactions, and system performance metrics.
    - **Debug Visualizers:** Use debugging tools to visualize the execution of code and the state of variables.
3. **Breakpoints and Stepping:**
    - Set breakpoints to pause execution at specific points in the code.
    - Step through code line by line to inspect variables and identify issues.
4. **Unit Testing:**

- Test individual agents in isolation to identify bugs and errors.
- Use unit testing frameworks to automate testing.

5. **Integration Testing:**
   - Test the integration of multiple agents to ensure they work together seamlessly.
   - Use simulation environments to test different scenarios and edge cases.
6. **A/B Testing:**
   - Test different configurations and algorithms to identify the best approach.
   - Use A/B testing to compare the performance of different versions of the system.

Debugging Strategies for Collaborative AI Systems:

- **Isolate Issues:** Identify the specific agent or component causing the issue.
- **Simplify the System:** Break down the system into smaller, more manageable components.
- **Use Debugging Tools:** Leverage debugging tools to inspect the state of the system.
- **Simulate Failures:** Simulate different failure scenarios to test the system's resilience.
- **Collaborate with Other Developers:** Seek help from other developers and experts.

Example: Debugging a Collaborative Robotics System

If a collaborative robot is not performing as expected, we can use the following debugging techniques:

- **Log Sensor Data:** Log sensor data to identify any anomalies or inconsistencies.
- **Visualize Robot Motion:** Use visualization tools to track the robot's movements and identify deviations from the desired trajectory.
- **Check Communication Logs:** Inspect communication logs to ensure that messages are being sent and received correctly.

- **Isolate Faulty Components:** Test individual components (e.g., sensors, actuators, controllers) to identify the root cause of the issue.

By effectively applying these debugging techniques, we can identify and resolve issues in CrewAI systems, ensuring their reliability and performance.

Chapter 18 Human-AI Collaboration

18.1 Designing Effective Human-AI Interfaces

Effective human-AI interfaces are crucial for seamless collaboration between humans and AI agents. A well-designed interface can enhance user experience, improve productivity, and foster trust in AI systems.

Key Principles for Designing Effective Human-AI Interfaces:

1. **User-Centered Design:**
   - Prioritize user needs and preferences.
   - Involve users in the design process to gather feedback.
   - Consider user experience factors like usability, learnability, and accessibility.
2. **Clear and Intuitive Interfaces:**
   - Use simple, intuitive interfaces that are easy to understand.
   - Avoid technical jargon and use clear, concise language.
   - Provide visual cues and feedback to guide users.
3. **Effective Communication:**
   - Design clear and concise communication protocols between humans and AI agents.
   - Use natural language processing to enable natural language interactions.
   - Provide timely and relevant feedback to users.
4. **Trust and Transparency:**
   - Be transparent about the capabilities and limitations of AI systems.
   - Explain the decision-making process of AI agents.
   - Build trust through consistent and reliable performance.
5. **Adaptability and Flexibility:**

- Design interfaces that can adapt to different user preferences and contexts.
- Allow users to customize the interface to their needs.

Understanding the User and Task

1. **User Research:**
   - Conduct user interviews and surveys to understand their needs, preferences, and technical expertise.
   - Create user personas to represent different types of users and their goals.
2. **Task Analysis:**
   - Break down complex tasks into smaller, more manageable subtasks.
   - Identify the specific roles of humans and AI agents in each task.

Designing the Interface

1. **Choose the Right Interface Type:**
   - **Command-line Interface (CLI):** Suitable for technical users who prefer text-based interactions.
   - **Graphical User Interface (GUI):** Suitable for general users who prefer visual interfaces.
   - **Natural Language Interface (NLI):** Enables natural language interactions, such as voice or text.
2. **Visual Design:**
   - Use clear and consistent visual elements, such as fonts, colors, and icons.
   - Design a layout that is easy to navigate and understand.
   - Consider the user's cognitive load and avoid information overload.
3. **Interaction Design:**
   - Design intuitive interactions that are easy to learn and use.
   - Provide clear feedback to users about their actions.
   - Implement error handling and recovery mechanisms.

Example: Designing a Voice-Activated Virtual Assistant

1. **User Research:** Identify target users and their primary use cases (e.g., setting alarms, playing music, answering questions).
2. **Natural Language Processing:** Develop a natural language processing model to understand and respond to user queries.
3. **Speech Recognition:** Implement speech recognition technology to convert spoken language into text.
4. **Text-to-Speech Synthesis:** Use text-to-speech technology to generate spoken responses.
5. **Design the Voice Interface:**
    - Use clear and concise prompts.
    - Provide feedback to the user to indicate that the command is being processed.
    - Handle errors and exceptions gracefully.

Additional Tips:

- **Iterative Design:** Continuously test and refine the interface based on user feedback.
- **Accessibility:** Design the interface to be accessible to users with disabilities.
- **Security and Privacy:** Protect user data and privacy.
- **Contextual Awareness:** Adapt the interface to the user's context and preferences.

Examples of Effective Human-AI Interfaces:

- **Voice Assistants:** Voice assistants like Siri, Alexa, and Google Assistant provide a natural and intuitive way to interact with AI.
- **Chatbots:** Chatbots can provide customer support, answer questions, and complete tasks.
- **Augmented Reality (AR) and Virtual Reality (VR):** AR and VR can be used to create immersive and interactive human-AI experiences.

By following these principles, we can design human-AI interfaces that are user-friendly, efficient, and effective.

18.2 Enhancing Human-AI Teamwork

Effective human-AI teamwork requires careful consideration of various factors to maximize the benefits of collaboration. Here are some key strategies to enhance human-AI teamwork:

1. Clear Roles and Responsibilities

- **Define roles:** Clearly define the roles of humans and AI agents in the collaborative process.
- **Allocate tasks:** Assign tasks based on the strengths and weaknesses of humans and AI.
- **Establish communication protocols:** Develop effective communication channels to facilitate collaboration.

2. Mutual Trust and Respect

- **Build trust:** Foster trust between humans and AI agents through transparency and reliability.
- **Respectful interaction:** Encourage respectful and collaborative behavior.
- **Avoid anthropomorphizing AI:** Avoid attributing human qualities to AI agents.

3. Continuous Learning and Adaptation

- **Human Learning:** Provide opportunities for humans to learn from AI agents, such as through explanations and visualizations.
- **AI Learning:** Enable AI agents to learn from human feedback and improve their performance.
- **Adaptive Systems:** Design systems that can adapt to changing circumstances and user preferences.

4. Ethical Considerations

- **Bias and Fairness:** Address biases in AI algorithms and data to ensure fair and equitable outcomes.
- **Privacy and Security:** Protect user privacy and data security.

- **Transparency:** Make AI systems transparent and explainable.

Real-World Example: Healthcare

In healthcare, human-AI teams can collaborate to improve patient outcomes. For example, a radiologist can work with an AI-powered image analysis system to detect tumors in medical images. The AI system can quickly analyze large amounts of data and highlight potential abnormalities, while the radiologist can interpret the results and make final decisions.

Key Strategies for Enhancing Teamwork in this Scenario:

- **Clear Communication:** The AI system should provide clear and concise explanations of its findings.
- **Human Oversight:** The radiologist should review and verify the AI system's recommendations.
- **Continuous Learning:** The AI system should be continuously trained and updated to improve its accuracy.
- **Ethical Considerations:** The AI system should be designed to protect patient privacy and avoid biases.

By effectively managing human-AI teamwork, we can unlock the full potential of AI and achieve significant benefits in various fields.

18.3 Leveraging Human Expertise to Improve AI Performance

Human expertise plays a crucial role in improving the performance and reliability of AI systems. By combining human intelligence with AI capabilities, we can create more powerful and effective solutions.

Key Strategies for Leveraging Human Expertise:

1. **Human-in-the-Loop:**
   - **Active Learning:** Humans can select the most informative data for training AI models.

- **Error Correction:** Humans can correct errors made by AI systems and provide feedback to improve performance.
- **Adversarial Testing:** Humans can design adversarial examples to test the robustness of AI systems.
2. **Human-AI Collaboration:**
    - **Shared Decision-Making:** Humans and AI agents can collaborate to make decisions.
    - **Task Allocation:** Humans can assign tasks to AI agents based on their capabilities.
    - **Feedback Loops:** Humans can provide feedback to AI agents to improve their performance.
3. **Explainable AI:**
    - **Model Interpretation:** Humans can interpret the decisions made by AI models.
    - **Visualization Techniques:** Visualize the decision-making process to gain insights.
    - **Counterfactual Explanations:** Explain how changes in input data would affect the model's output.

Real-World Example: Medical Diagnosis

In medical diagnosis, AI systems can analyze medical images, such as X-rays and CT scans, to identify potential abnormalities. However, human radiologists are still essential for interpreting the results and making final diagnoses. By combining the strengths of both humans and AI, medical professionals can improve the accuracy and efficiency of diagnoses.

Key Benefits of Human-AI Collaboration:

- **Improved Performance:** Humans can provide valuable insights and feedback to improve AI performance.
- **Increased Trust and Transparency:** Human involvement can help build trust in AI systems.
- **Ethical Considerations:** Humans can ensure that AI systems are used ethically and responsibly.

By effectively leveraging human expertise, we can create AI systems that are more reliable, accurate, and aligned with human values.

Chapter 19: The Future of Collaborative AI and CrewAI

19.1 Trends in AI Collaboration and Future Applications

As AI technology continues to evolve, we can expect to see significant advancements in the field of collaborative AI. Some of the key trends shaping the future of CrewAI include:

1. Increased Complexity and Scalability

- **Large-Scale Collaboration:** AI systems will be able to collaborate on increasingly complex tasks, involving a large number of agents.
- **Scalable Infrastructure:** Cloud-based platforms and distributed computing will enable the scaling of CrewAI systems to handle massive amounts of data and computations.

2. Enhanced Human-AI Collaboration

- **Natural Language Interfaces:** AI systems will become more adept at understanding and responding to natural language, facilitating seamless human-AI interaction.
- **Augmented Intelligence:** AI will augment human capabilities, enabling us to make better decisions and solve complex problems.

3. Ethical AI and Responsible Development

- **Fairness and Bias Mitigation:** AI systems will be designed to be fair and unbiased.
- **Privacy and Security:** Strong measures will be implemented to protect user privacy and data security.
- **Transparency and Explainability:** AI systems will be more transparent and explainable, fostering trust and understanding.

4. AI for Social Good

- **Healthcare:** AI will revolutionize healthcare by enabling early disease detection, personalized treatment plans, and drug discovery.
- **Education:** AI-powered personalized learning systems will enhance educational outcomes.
- **Environmental Conservation:** AI can help monitor environmental changes, predict natural disasters, and develop sustainable solutions.

Future Applications

- **Autonomous Systems:** AI-powered autonomous systems, such as self-driving cars and drones, will become more sophisticated and widespread.
- **Smart Cities:** AI will enable the creation of smart cities with efficient transportation, energy management, and public services.
- **Human Augmentation:** AI can enhance human capabilities, such as improving cognitive abilities and physical performance.

As CrewAI technology continues to advance, we can expect to see even more innovative and impactful applications that will shape the future of our society.

19.2 Innovations and Emerging Technologies in CrewAI

The field of CrewAI is rapidly evolving, with several innovative technologies and techniques emerging on the horizon. Here are some of the most promising developments:

1. Reinforcement Learning and Multi-Agent Reinforcement Learning

- **Training Complex Behaviors:** Reinforcement learning enables AI agents to learn optimal strategies through trial and error, making them suitable for complex tasks like autonomous navigation and game playing.

- **Collaborative Learning:** Multi-agent reinforcement learning allows multiple agents to learn and coordinate their actions, leading to more effective and robust systems.

2. Generative AI

- **Creative Content Generation:** Generative AI models can generate creative content, such as text, images, and music.
- **Design and Innovation:** AI can assist in the design and prototyping of new products and services.

3. Explainable AI

- **Model Interpretability:** Explainable AI techniques help to understand the decision-making process of AI models, increasing trust and transparency.
- **Fairness and Bias Mitigation:** Explainable AI can be used to identify and mitigate biases in AI systems.

4. Edge AI

- **Real-Time Processing:** Edge AI enables AI processing to be performed on devices at the edge of the network, reducing latency and improving privacy.
- **Distributed Intelligence:** Edge AI can distribute intelligence across multiple devices, creating more robust and resilient systems.

5. Quantum Computing

- **Accelerated AI:** Quantum computing has the potential to accelerate AI computations, enabling the development of more sophisticated AI models.
- **Quantum Machine Learning:** Quantum machine learning algorithms can solve complex problems that are intractable for classical computers.

These emerging technologies will further enhance the capabilities of CrewAI systems, enabling them to tackle more complex and challenging tasks. As AI continues to advance, we can expect to see even more innovative and impactful applications of CrewAI in the future.

19.3 How to Stay Updated on Advances in Collaborative AI

To stay up-to-date with the latest advancements in collaborative AI, consider the following strategies:

1. Follow Leading Researchers and Organizations

- **Academic Institutions:** Keep an eye on research papers and publications from renowned universities like Stanford, MIT, and UC Berkeley.
- **Industry Leaders:** Follow the work of leading AI companies like Google, Microsoft, OpenAI, and Meta.
- **AI Conferences and Workshops:** Attend conferences like NeurIPS, ICML, and ICLR to learn about the latest research and trends.

2. Leverage Online Resources

- **Research Papers:** Explore online repositories like arXiv to access the latest research papers.
- **Blogs and Websites:** Follow AI blogs and websites, such as Towards Data Science, Machine Learning Mastery, and the blogs of leading AI companies.
- **Social Media:** Follow AI researchers and organizations on social media platforms like Twitter and LinkedIn.

3. Participate in Online Communities

- **Forums and Communities:** Join online forums and communities like Reddit's r/MachineLearning and Kaggle to discuss ideas and learn from others.
- **Online Courses and Tutorials:** Take online courses on platforms like Coursera, edX, and Udacity to learn new skills and techniques.

4. Experiment and Build Projects

- **Hands-on Experience:** Experiment with AI tools and frameworks to gain practical experience.
- **Open-Source Projects:** Contribute to open-source AI projects to learn from other developers and collaborate on innovative ideas.

5. Stay Curious and Keep Learning

- **Continuous Learning:** Stay curious and keep learning about new technologies and techniques.
- **Embrace Lifelong Learning:** Attend workshops, webinars, and conferences to stay updated on the latest trends.

By following these strategies, you can stay informed about the latest advancements in collaborative AI and position yourself to contribute to the future of this exciting field.

19.4 Final Thoughts on CrewAI for Beginners

As you embark on your journey into the world of CrewAI, remember that the key to success lies in understanding the fundamental principles, experimenting with different techniques, and collaborating with others.

Key Takeaways:

- **Collaboration is Key:** Effective communication and coordination among AI agents are essential for achieving desired outcomes.
- **Data is the Fuel:** High-quality data is crucial for training and fine-tuning AI models.
- **Continuous Learning:** AI systems should be continuously learning and adapting to new information and challenges.
- **Ethical Considerations:** Always consider the ethical implications of AI and strive to develop systems that are fair, transparent, and beneficial to society.
- **Experimentation and Innovation:** Be open to experimentation and embrace new ideas to push the boundaries of AI.

Future of CrewAI:

The future of CrewAI is bright, with exciting possibilities on the horizon. We can expect to see significant advancements in:

- **Autonomous Systems:** Self-driving cars, drones, and robots will become more sophisticated and capable.
- **Healthcare:** AI-powered tools will revolutionize medical diagnosis, drug discovery, and personalized treatment.
- **Climate Change:** AI can help us understand and mitigate climate change by analyzing large datasets and optimizing energy consumption.
- **Education:** AI-powered personalized learning systems will transform education.

By staying informed about the latest trends and actively participating in the AI community, you can contribute to the development of innovative and beneficial CrewAI systems. Remember, the future of AI is in your hands!

Appendix

A.1 Glossary of Key Terms

Agent: An autonomous entity that can perceive its environment, make decisions, and take actions.

Artificial Intelligence (AI): The science of making intelligent machines, especially intelligent computer programs.

Machine Learning (ML): A subset of AI that involves training algorithms on data to make predictions or decisions.

Deep Learning: A subset of ML that uses artificial neural networks with multiple layers to learn complex patterns.

Natural Language Processing (NLP): A field of AI that focuses on the interaction between computers and human language.

Computer Vision: A field of AI that enables computers to interpret and understand visual information from the world.

Reinforcement Learning: A type of ML where agents learn to make decisions by interacting with an environment and receiving rewards or penalties.

CrewAI: A collaborative AI system that involves multiple AI agents working together to solve complex problems.

Task Allocation: The process of assigning tasks to agents based on their capabilities and workload.

Communication Protocol: A set of rules and procedures for exchanging information between agents.

Data Sharing: The process of sharing data between agents to enable collaboration and decision-making.

Agent Specialization: The process of assigning specific roles and responsibilities to different agents.

Workflow Management: The process of organizing and coordinating the tasks and activities of AI agents.

Human-AI Collaboration: The interaction between humans and AI agents to achieve a common goal.

Bias and Fairness: The ethical consideration of ensuring that AI systems are unbiased and fair.

Privacy and Security: The protection of sensitive information and data privacy.

Explainable AI: The development of AI models that can explain their decision-making processes.

A.2 Additional Resources and Recommended Reading

To delve deeper into the world of CrewAI, consider exploring the following resources:

Online Courses and Tutorials

- **Coursera:** Offers a wide range of AI and machine learning courses, including deep learning, reinforcement learning, and natural language processing.
- **edX:** Provides various AI and machine learning courses, often in collaboration with top universities.
- **Udacity:** Offers practical, project-based courses on AI, machine learning, and data science.
- **Kaggle:** A platform for data science competitions and learning, where you can practice your skills and learn from others.

Books

- **Artificial Intelligence: A Modern Approach** by Stuart Russell and Peter Norvig

- **Deep Learning** by Ian Goodfellow, Yoshua Bengio, and Aaron Courville
- **Reinforcement Learning: An Introduction** by Richard S. Sutton and Andrew G. Barto
- **Hands-On Machine Learning with Scikit-Learn, Keras, and TensorFlow** by Aurélien Géron

Research Papers and Preprint Servers

- **arXiv:** A preprint server for physics, mathematics, computer science, and other scientific disciplines.
- **Google Scholar:** A search engine for scholarly literature.
- **ACM Digital Library:** A digital library of computer science publications.
- **IEEE Xplore:** A digital library of IEEE publications.

Open-Source Frameworks and Libraries

- **TensorFlow:** A popular open-source platform for machine learning and deep learning.
- **PyTorch:** A flexible and efficient deep learning framework.
- **Scikit-learn:** A powerful machine learning library for Python.
- **OpenAI Gym:** A toolkit for developing and comparing reinforcement learning algorithms.

AI Research Labs and Organizations

- **OpenAI:** A leading AI research lab focused on developing and promoting friendly AI.
- **Google AI:** Google's AI research division, working on a wide range of AI projects.
- **Microsoft Research:** Microsoft's research division, focused on AI, machine learning, and other cutting-edge technologies.

- **Facebook AI Research (FAIR):** Facebook's AI research lab, working on areas like computer vision, natural language processing, and reinforcement learning.

By leveraging these resources, you can stay updated on the latest advancements in CrewAI and contribute to the development of innovative AI solutions.

A.3 Index

Part I: Foundations of CrewAI

- Chapter 1: Introduction to CrewAI
- Chapter 2: Core Concepts of Artificial Intelligence
- Chapter 3: Building Blocks of CrewAI Systems

Part II: Designing and Developing CrewAI Systems

- Chapter 4: Defining Goals and Requirements
- Chapter 5: Creating Task Flows and Agent Architectures
- Chapter 6: Communication and Task Coordination
- Chapter 7: Data Sharing and Processing
- Chapter 8: Agent Role Specialization
- Chapter 9: Workflow Management
- Chapter 10: Conflict Resolution

Part III: Advanced Topics in CrewAI

- Chapter 11: Training and Improving AI Agents
- Chapter 12: CrewAI in Business and Industry
- Chapter 13: Advanced Use Cases in Research and Development
- Chapter 14: Developing Custom CrewAI Solutions
- Chapter 15: Best Practices for CrewAI Success
- Chapter 16: Ethical and Social Considerations

Appendix

1. A.1 Glossary of Key Terms
2. A.2 Additional Resources and Recommended Reading
3. A.3 Index

Conclusion

As we've explored the intricacies of CrewAI, it's clear that this technology has the potential to revolutionize industries and solve some of the world's most pressing challenges. By understanding the fundamental concepts, mastering the techniques, and considering the ethical implications, you can contribute to the development of intelligent, collaborative systems that benefit society.

This book has provided a solid foundation for your journey into the world of CrewAI. Remember, the future of AI is collaborative, and by embracing this paradigm, we can unlock unprecedented opportunities and create a better future for all.

So, dive deeper, experiment, and innovate. Let your imagination soar as you explore the limitless possibilities of CrewAI. Share your knowledge, inspire others, and become a part of the future of AI.